"Too many parents think, "My kid gets good grades, doesn't do drugs and gets home by curfew so I'm a good parent. WRONG!"

—Your child?

What I Wish You Knew:

Conversations with Teens

Sharon Weingarten, MSW

with

Mariana Glusman, MD

Victoria Sandler, MD, Laura Thompson

and students all over the world

What I Wish You Knew Press
Northbrook, Illinois

For Judy

Dedication

To the memories of Dr. Sophie Levinson, Dr. Robert Gluckman, Alex Glusman, Joan Thompson, and Monette Park of Columbine High School.

And to all the young people who generously shared their advice, time and passion for this project. You were my inspiration. **What I Wish You Knew Conversations** would have never happened without you. I was, and continue to be, touched and impressed by your commitment. You gathered to discuss our book and website in dorm rooms and classrooms, in coffee shops and in meetings at my dining room table. You participated in professional workshops in schools, hospitals and libraries. You taught me the importance of asking good questions. You shared your honest and heartfelt feelings unselfconsciously, and you gave advice about what parents would benefit from knowing. Because of you, parents and other adults will learn skills to help them have meaningful conversations with their children.

As promised, I did not reveal names with your writings. But take a look at the Acknowledgments page at the end of the book. You know who you are! Never underestimate the impact your words will have in families. As promised, proceeds of this book will be donated to charities you choose.

"What I Wish You Knew Conversations is extremely important because it provides a means by which a parent and child can communicate more easily and more comfortably with each other. It is difficult for parents and teens to talk about subjects that have social, emotional and conflictual components. You don't have to hit a subject 'head on' or 'point blank.'

The unique approach of this book, encouraging discussion of the words of a third party, makes many subjects easier to talk about and has the ability to open conversations of substance. Parents and their children are given the opportunity for both listening to, and respecting, one another. When teens and parents communicate, they are not only expressing themselves to each other, but are given the opportunity to understand the feelings behind the words. This approach is a wonderful idea. *What I Wish You Knew Conversations* will be extremely helpful for parents who want better communication with their children. It is sure to initiate conversations in families."

Robert Gluckman, MD, Emeritus
Northwestern University Medical School
American Academy of Child Psychiatry

"Interested in understanding what your teen really thinks? *What I Wish You Knew Conversations* may be of help. Written by Sharon Weingarten, a sensitive and observant clinician and mother, this book offers an illuminating look into the inner world of adolescents.

Teens naturally (and understandably) keep much to themselves as they develop identities and lives independent of their parents. Supporting and guiding them through this process takes patience, a bit of wisdom, and the ability to truly listen to your teens' thoughts, feelings, and concerns. In this slim volume you'll listen in on teens lives as they share their worries

Mark A. Reinecke, PhD
Professor & Chief Psychologist
Northwestern University

"Being involved in this process and seeing how kids are being listened to and taken seriously was transforming and empowering for me. I discussed a lot of the quotes with my mom. It was great. I can't wait till these are all put into the book. I want to give one to my cousin. Maybe this will help her and her mom at least be able to talk about some things, instead of always fighting about everything."

Student

"… What is brilliant about this book is that the teens' voices resonate with other teens, creating a natural opening for discussion. Teens have a lot on their minds that they don't tell their parents. As a pediatrician, I see every day teens that succeed and teens that get in trouble. I am convinced that those that have good relationships with at least one adult do better. As a parent, I know how hard it is to let kids become independent, knowing that there are risks and that sometimes you have to let them make their own mistakes. Staying 'in the loop' is the best way to keep them safe. ***What I Wish You Knew Conversations*** is full of fascinating, sweet, sad, and even scary comments from teens. I encourage any adult that lives, loves or works with teens to read this book and share it with them. An adult, or a teen, can chose a page, or a chapter or a comment to talk about. I plan to be using them as openers in future conversations with my patients and especially with my own teens!

Mariana Glusman, MD

"What parents aren't told by their own children, they should hear from us, the kids in the book.

I jumped at the chance to help with this project. I worked on it because it seemed tragic to me that so many teenagers, who more than likely told their parents they were "fine," had poured out their hearts to someone else. Since they had the courage to speak their true thoughts, I was willing to help them be heard on an even broader scale. Everyone should be heard, even moody teenagers who walk in the door silently, run up to their rooms, and slam the door.

Adults often forget the pressure society puts on teens to figure out who they are, and the anxiety that accompanies trying to have such an epiphany before making more than a handful of decisions on their own. I wanted to help with this project because I realized that teenagers have to communicate with parents a little better. We need to help them listen to us.

I think that maybe parents trivialize things that are important to us because they don't even know what they are. We are immersed in a culture that parents don't understand.

Although well-intentioned parents assume that teaching good values can protect their children from making bad choices, teens today exist in an increasingly dangerous world with total mobility and no judgment.

Parents, here are real kids telling you what you probably aren't hearing from your own children. They are telling you what they wish you knew - and even giving you advice on how you can help.

As someone who survived adolescence unscathed, I attribute this accomplishment to the generosity of the adults that gave me their time and attention as I attempted to sort out the world."

"How are parents to know the details of their teens' lives? I participated in this project because I know firsthand that parents should be reading these words.

Some of the pages that follow (that might have been written by your child) give older generations a sense of what it is like to be an adolescent in current times. For parents, reading the words of today's youth is like listening in on our conversations and having the opportunity to know some of the things that are on our minds. It's like a universal diary key to understanding a little about our lives. Hopefully, some parents will read my words and discuss them with their child. Then more families might not be saying, 'If only we had known...'

The reality of parent-teen interactions today is that there are no distinct rules that govern what is normal and what is dangerous. Many parents search for the universal key to understanding, which turns out not to exist, and thus they are unable to hear their child's sometimes silent call for help.

I heard the story of a girl who committed suicide. One evening my family had the opportunity to meet her family. We learned that she was a kind and intelligent person, who still was unsatisfied enough with herself to take her own life. I, too, had many things going for me but I also was really stressed. As we talked with this other family, it became clear to my parents that young adult stress is a very serious issue. Later that evening, my mother repeated the phrase that the other parents used in talking about their daughter, 'If only someone had known...'

p.s.
In addition to what you are reading on this page, I wrote something else in the book. At the time I wrote it I did not realize the implications of putting down my thoughts on paper. But maybe my writing will help some parent to help their own child.

    My boyfriend asked me why I would help with this book when I wasn't being paid for it. He completely understood when I explained my reasoning: because I wish my mom and dad had a book on how to listen to me when I was a teenager.

I'm a few years out of my teenage-hood, but I do remember how frustrating it was to try to explain my life to someone and not be able to finish or clarify or re-explain my thoughts and feelings. I have a 17-year-old brother and catch myself brushing off his concerns and worries as needless and exaggerated. Teenagers rarely have life-or-death problems, right? Well, unfortunately, teenagers are having more responsibilities and pressures (college, financial aid, sex, depression, divorced-parent-wars, etc.) put on their shoulders at younger ages so previously managed problems can become life threatening. Ask any teenager. I'll bet they know someone who has talked about suicide or is on anti-depressants.

The battle between teenagers and adults has been waged since "teenager" was first coined. The difference now is we have the "me" generation of parents raising the "me" generation of teenagers, and both think they know it all. Teenagers need to be taught and guided to be good adults, but the only way to do so is to first understand who they are as individuals, who they want to be and how they want to get there. And how do we do that? Listen.

Parents, you have to listen. Most of the time, there is nothing you can do except give your son or daughter a hug and say you understand, share a similar story, and reassure her things will work out. I spent years teaching myself that the world would not end if I made a mistake. It resulted in a tattoo of the sun on my hip, and each morning as I get dressed I remind myself, 'No matter what happens today the sun will still rise tomorrow.'

Table of Contents

Foreword

Mariana Glusman, MD

As a pediatrician I have had thousands of conversations with teens. It's pretty amazing how candid they can be as soon as their parents step out of the room. They tell me, confidentially, about arguments with parents, "drama" with their friends, school problems, bullying, relationships, sex, drugs… I encourage them to talk with their parents, but I know that many times they won't.

I have also had thousands of conversations with parents of teens. But they are so similar that it feels like one big conversation. Parents worry about their teens, sometimes with good reason. They struggle with how to give them independence and at the same time keep them safe and teach them to be responsible adults. I am going through the same thing with my own kids, two teens and a 'tween. They have taught me, and everyday remind me, how hard it is to be a parent! I've also had, and continue to have, conversations with my friends about how to interact with our own teens. We all struggle with the same questions:

How open should I be?

How do I get them to open up to me?

How tolerant should I be?

What surgical instrument do I use to separate them from the screen (TV, computer, video-games, Ipad, phone…)?

How can I motivate them to do their homework?

How much freedom (to go out/to be with friends/to drive/to stay out late/to go to parties/etc.) should I give them?

Is it better to have them drink/smoke in my house rather than in someone else's (or in the alley)?

How do I talk with them about sex/birth control/drugs?

How do I keep them safe?

Some things are universal. As parents, we want so much for our kids, most of all we want them to be safe and healthy and happy. So it is painful to see them not living up to their potential, having conflicts with friends, getting involved in hurtful relationships, engaging in risky behaviors. But kids do stupid things. We all did, in one way or another. Some things they have to go through on their own.

Nevertheless, despite the façade of independence, most teens do want their parents to be involved, and to set limits. Parenting a teen is one big negotiation with lots of pushing and pulling. However, there are many differences between this new generation of teens and previous generations.

Easier access to drugs and alcohol

More acceptance of sex without intimacy

More access to technology and 24/7 connections

More academic pressure. It feels as if in order to get into some colleges now, you have to have founded an orphanage, been a star athlete, and played an instrument while getting perfect grades!

More pressure about the future. Getting a job is harder than before.

There is also a higher awareness about teasing and bullying and their harmful short and long-term effects.

Most teens do well. But the above factors can lead to stress, poor school performance, illnesses such as headaches and abdominal pains, depression and even suicidal ideation. It is now more important than ever to have open lines of communication with our teens to help them navigate through these dangerous obstacles.

In order to have these kinds of conversations, the context has to be safe and the tone non-judgmental. It also helps to start with someone else's experience and slowly let the discussion turn more personal. For instance, I mentioned to my 15 year-old son, that one of the teens in this book had written, "My parents have no idea how easy it is to get drugs in school." He quickly answered, "Yes, about one in three kids in my school smokes pot." I asked him if they did it often and when, before school? And he said, "Mom, I don't know their drug schedules, I don't smoke with them!" We talked a little bit about how he felt about it…. and how I felt about it. I didn't ask him to tell me which of his friends smoke; I didn't drill him. We just talked. Our conversation lasted at most five minutes. It was casual and relaxed. Although I hate that he has such easy access to drugs, I know that is the case in many high schools. Seeing that I didn't react in a negative way reinforced to him that it's ok to tell me things, and hopefully he will continue to do so in the future.

Creating the Setting for Conversations

There is often the discussion of quality time vs. quantity time. I believe that quality time is very difficult to get without quantity time. Very few people, not just teens, will react well if you say to them, "We have to talk."

Most parents will tell you that some of the best conversations they've had with their kids occurred in the car, driving to or from some activity or errand. There are no distractions, other than traffic, and I wonder if there is something to the fact that you are not looking directly at them, so the conversation feels more casual.

Also, conversations need to be light sometimes. It is helpful to remember the 5 to 1 rule (5 positive topics to 1 negative or "heavy" topic). And adults need to demonstrate genuine interest in what teens have to say. *What I Wish You Knew Conversations* provides an excellent tool to start and continue conversations with teens. Over the past ten years Sharon Weingarten has collected writings by teens on many topics, but specifically giving advice to parents. In compiling them into this book, she gives us insight into what teens are thinking and experiencing. The comments remind me of what teens tell me in our confidential conversations, when their parents step out of the exam room. But what is brilliant about this book is that the teens' voices resonate with other teens, creating a natural opening for discussion.

Lastly, one must keep in mind the different stages of teen development. Often we talk about "teens" as if there were all in one developmental stage (like toddlers). But there is a world of difference between a thirteen and a nineteen year-old! According to the American Academy of Pediatrics, adolescent development can be divided into three stages: early (11-13 year olds), middle (14-17 year olds) and late adolescence (18-21 year olds). Different kids will go through these stages at different ages, but the patterns tend to remain the same. Along with the physical changes that take place during adolescence, there are important cognitive and socio-emotional milestones that need to be achieved in the transition from childhood to adulthood. (The following descriptions are adapted from the American Academy of Child and Adolescent Psychiatry: Facts for Families, 2008).

Early adolescence (11-13 years)

As puberty begins, accompanied by rapid growth and increased sexual interest, young teens begin to feel awkward, and conflicted about their sense of identity. They feel embarrassed and self-conscious about the changes in their bodies and worry that they may not be normal. Their peer groups become more influential, and they begin to realize that their parents are far from perfect. It has been widely noted that early teens and toddlers-preschoolers have a lot in common:

- They want to be independent but are ambivalent about it

- They have temper tantrums

- They feel that the world revolves around them

- They have "imaginary" friends (remember middle school?)

- They test rules and limits

But at the same time, early teens develop a growing capacity for abstract thought and their intellectual interests expand. While they still tend to be rooted in the present, they start to have deeper moral understanding. Early teens can be emotional and "childish," but they are also delightful and earnest, they are better able to argue and practice that skill frequently. They question the rules and begin to push boundaries, at home, in school and in society at large.

Middle Adolescence (14-17 years)

Pubertal changes slow down for girls and continue for most boys, but the issues of adjustment to changing bodies and their worries about being normal persist. They can have abrupt shifts between high expectations and poor self-concept. They desperately want to be independent and may actively distance themselves from their parents. The opinions of their peers are enormously important and they are deeply affected by issues of social status and popularity. While teens at this stage can be intensely self-absorbed they also develop feelings of love and passion. Middle adolescents have an increased capacity for abstract thought and a growing interest in moral reasoning. They are passionate and idealistic which is wonderful in some situations, but can also lead to big disappointments and feelings of inadequacy and poor self-esteem.

Late Adolescence (18-21 years)

Physical development for both males and females is typically completed by this age, though young men may continue to gain height, weight and muscle mass. At this stage, executive functioning is better developed and they are able to think ideas through. Coinciding with high school graduation, they have an increased concern for the future, as well as increased self-reliance and independence. While relationships remain important, they develop a firmer sense of identity and have less emotional volatility. Their moral reasoning continues to expand along with their concern for others. They develop more serious relationships and social and cultural traditions regain some of their importance. With increased maturity, late adolescents are poised to start their own independent lives as young adults.

Each of these stages brings new joys and new frustrations. Knowing these different stages can help parents and other adults that interact with teens to have appropriate expectations. For example, it makes no sense for a mom to get angry at her nine month old because he can't walk yet, and no amount of training or help will make him walk earlier. On the other hand, this mom can make the environment safer so that as the infant starts to walk he will not bump into things that will make him fall, and when he falls he lands on a rug instead of concrete. Similarly, it is not reasonable to expect that a 15 year-old will make consistently rational decisions, such as not drinking alcohol at parties. On the other hand, parents can make the environment safe, for instance, make sure the party is supervised by adults so that he is less tempted to make bad choices, and pick him up after the party so that, if he does drink, at least he does not get in a car with a drunk driver. In both instances, for toddlers and teens, having concerned and involved parents helps kids feel secure so they can move on to their next stage of development.

Introduction

"How do I get my children to talk to me?"

"My kids don't listen."

"What in the world is going on with kids today?"

"Is there a time of day that is better or worse try to have a conversation with my teenager?"

Your kids don't talk to you? I've heard that a lot. I have also heard,

***"**I can't talk to my parents. Why bother? They never listen. They feel they either have to be imparting wisdom or grilling me about my friends. They supposedly want to know about my life and my problems, but it's impossible to have a real conversation with them. We never just talk. It's easier to just say everything is fine."*

What I Wish You Knew Conversations was created with the simple goal of fostering better communication in families by encouraging more frequent "little" conversations so that there might be less need for "big" ones. It is my observation that people we care about can be compared to our pulse. Usually we don't pay much attention unless something seems wrong.

And then we have to pay a <u>LOT</u> of attention!

Too often it's not until it's too late that we realize how very important it is to be "tuned in" to our kids.

Communicating before problems occur could help prevent a lot of the problems.

From working with adolescents for over 25 years, I know how much they have on their minds. Some have shared stories with me and then asked me to talk to their parents for them. Better they learn how to do that themselves. They have a lot to say and really do want to be heard.

After all the listening to both teens and parents talk about their concerns and interviewing hundreds of teens about things that matter to them, my best advice to parents is to try to get your child to share what's on his mind with you and then listen, listen, listen. But I know it is not easy, especially the getting your child to share part.

Too often what starts out as an opportunity to talk turns into questions that are answered in monosyllables.

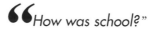

"How was school?"

"OK"

There is a lot of talk about the importance of keeping the lines of communication open. But that is so much easier said than done. It's not that we don't want to talk with each other; it's that we don't know how - and we don't know when. Everyone is so busy. We put it off until we find just the right time and that never seems to come. Or, what passes for real communication takes the form of some variation of,

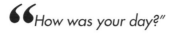**How was your day?"**

Fine"

Good"

Read what this high school student had to say when asked about the frequent use of the word, FINE.

66*There is no day that can honestly be described as fine. 'Fine' is usually delivered with the misleading teenage tone of voice that covers uncertainties and insecurities with outrage and anger. The tone of voice that accosts the listener, even in a single word, with the questions, 'Why are you asking me this? Why don't you just leave me alone?' 'Fine' is a mask. 'Fine' hides a C- on a recent physics test, a heart-stopping smile from the cute boy with the locker across the hall and a fight with a friend that feels like the end of the world. Parents and kids may have a lot in common, probably more than either is willing to admit, but growing up today is not the same as it was a generation ago. Our days are a lot more than just FINE."*

How it Began

The idea for What I Wish You Knew Conversations was born from a personal experience. Many years ago when one of my own children was in college at the University of Queensland, my husband and I experienced every parent's nightmare. We received a call telling us that our daughter had been seriously injured in an accident. I was on the next flight to Australia. Fortunately, the injury was not life-threatening, but it did require a prolonged period of bed rest and recuperation. Because the doctors advised against her taking the twenty-hour flight back home right away, the plan was that after her release from the hospital she would return to the University, where she would rest and have physical therapy while she recuperated. I was allowed to stay in one of the empty rooms in her dormitory until she was able to travel.

During that time I had the opportunity to experience something that most mothers don't. For over a month, knowing that my husband was at home taking care of our other two children, I was undistracted by normal demands of home, family, work and other responsibilities. I was living in a girl's dorm on the other side of the world and had the luxury of not having to multi-task, of really being able to live in the moment, to be there for my child and to think. I also had the opportunity to get to know many students.

The kids were kind and helpful and curious and forthright too. After a while, I stopped being a strange phenomenon and they began to accept me. They told me about their "mums" and about other things too. They asked questions and talked about their lives and gave me some advice to pass on to other parents.

One of the things they told me about was a friend who took her own life earlier that year. They told me about her parents who said, "If only we had known what she was going through…" and "If only she had talked to us and confided in us…"

A lot of what the kids shared was their desire to be able to talk more easily with their own parents. Probably because I was not their own mother and because there was a degree of anonymity in talking with me around, they did so easily. I was just like a fly on the wall.

Being respectful of what they had to say and of their privacy, I created www.whatiwishyouknew.com for them to have a safe place to express their thoughts and ideas and opinions. I have had the privilege of communicating with teens from around the world. I have since interviewed hundreds more students in classrooms, in libraries, in a homeless shelter, in youth agencies, and, through an interpreter in a school for the deaf.

In addition, through my work with WorldTeach, I had the opportunity to introduce the What I Wish You Knew Conversations writing project in schools in the Pacific Islands.

Collective Journal

No matter their age or where they live, most teens simply want to be heard and taken seriously. And they want to be able to talk with their parents more easily. They feel that adults don't have any idea of the pressures they have; that they don't appreciate how much times have changed in recent years, and that even the most well-intentioned parents have a lot to learn.

> 66 *Too many parents think, 'My kid gets good grades, doesn't do drugs and gets home by curfew so I'm a good parent.' WRONG!!"*

They shared their honest and heartfelt feelings unselfconsciously and were eager to give advice about what parents would benefit from knowing. All the students interviewed wanted to help adults realize the importance of taking the time to really listen to their children.

> 66 *Sometimes it feels like a daily battle just to survive. We need well-informed adults to tune in. Parents should step away from the articles on parenting and self-help books they're always reading and start to listen to us, the actual kids."*

The results of hundreds of interviews that you are about to read have been gathered for over a decade and come from a wide variety of students. Children who are blessed with good health and some who are not, kids in public schools and some in private or special needs schools, teens from cities, suburbs and small communities tell parents and other adults what they think and feel and worry about.

I CREATED THIS BOOK TO GIVE VOICE TO TEENS WHO TOO OFTEN KEEP THEIR FEELINGS TO THEMSELVES.

HOWEVER, ALTHOUGH THEY WANT ADULTS TO UNDERSTAND MORE ABOUT THEIR LIVES, THEY DON'T WANT TO SIT ACROSS THE TABLE FROM THEIR PARENTS AND HAVE A CONVERSATION WITH THEM ABOUT THEIR PERSONAL PROBLEMS.

IT IS A LOT EASIER TO TALK ABOUT OTHER PEOPLE AND <u>THEIR PROBLEMS</u>.

Many of the students said that they "would have died" if their parents had read their real diaries. But in this Collective Journal they offer parents, teachers and other adults the gifts of knowing more about their children's lives and hearing them tell us what they want and need.

Although names do not appear, very real kids welcomed the opportunity to write advice or letters to their parents. Not unlike the maids in Kathryn Stockett's "The Help," the people who shared their feelings here felt more comfortable knowing that they were promised anonymity. Some of the quotes will appear more than once throughout this book. This is not by accident or error, but very purposeful. These were opinions that were shared several times.

How to Use This Book

What I Wish You Knew Conversations is a deceptively simple way of launching conversations though the voices of others. It can help parents get to know their children a lot better without being "in their face." It can also help students initiate communication with their parents about important topics. Too often "a talk" means a parent lectures and a teen rolls his eyes.

The pages that follow help families move beyond that and enable parents to take the "emotional pulse" of their child. I advise parents to do this often and not wait until something is wrong. Students agree.

> **"***Parents shouldn't just wait till their child gets pregnant or quits school or is arrested.*"

When parents ask, "How do I get my kids to really open up to me?" my response is to stop talking AT your children and begin to spend more time talking WITH them. Use the pages that follow, not for "The Big Talk," but rather just as openers for frequent, easy, conversations. It is a lot easier to have Big Talks if you have experience talking about a variety of other things <u>with</u> each other. Note WITH, not AT each other.

Directions

Directions couldn't be simpler. Each section of this book includes opportunities for initiating important conversations, either by discussing some of the writings or by answering the Starters questions in the Introduction.

Some of the quotes are very short, but like a good New Yorker cartoon, the point will be obvious. Just choose a page and share it with your child. Or let your teen look through the book and pick a page about an issue that interests him and ask, "What do you think about this?" There are no right answers and there is no right order. Each page is simply intended to be a talking point.

Your child may tell you that the writing on the page is stupid, but most kids will respond if you ask them WHY they think it is stupid. He won't get defensive because the writing is not about him. It's about what someone else expressed. Discussing someone else's problem or opinion takes the focus off your child and makes the issue easier to talk about.

You and your child might have the same opinion about the issues presented and you might not. But having the same opinion is not the goal; the goal is to just talk about the issue on the page, not AT or about each other.

The goal is simply to practice communicating respectfully. The process is easy and a surprisingly effective way to get to know each other better. Here's how:

- Listen to your teen as he tells you his response to what he is reading as if he were talking about his response to an image in a Rorschach Test.

- Reply to what he has to say with respect and curiosity. Don't interrupt or offer advice or try to change his mind.

- Listen with patience and respect, the way you want him to listen to others, the way you want him to listen to you. You are letting him know that you are interested in HIM and what he thinks.

- Give him time to answer. There are not right answers or wrong responses, just the sharing of opinions.

- Respond to what he has to say as you would to someone else - someone you don't love.

- Ask your child about what topics he thinks are missing, subjects that should have been included.

- Ask him what he thinks of the student who wrote the quote. Can he relate to the writer? Does he know anyone who has a problem like that?

- Ask your child what she wishes she could tell the writer's parents?

- Share (briefly) how the page makes you feel and what you would like to say to the student who wrote it.

- Wonder (to yourself or aloud) if your child might have been someone who contributed to this book.

- Talk about just one page or more than one. Each of you can respond to the same writing or choose different pages to think about. You can involve other members of the family in these discussions, or not. There is no right or wrong way to use this book. Just do whatever works for you.

Another option is to use some of the writings in the book to journal. You and your child (or just one of you) can write your thoughts and opinions about some of the writings in the book. Then share your responses with one another if you choose.

Remember this is not a "how to" book, but rather just a guide, so that you can practice having frequent, easy and respectful conversations in your family. That's it, just a simple (and maybe new) way to talk with your child and learn more about her and what she thinks in a non-emotional and non-judgmental way.

Most teens feel pleasantly surprised that you aren't "imparting wisdom" or "grilling" them. When they get used to it and begin to trust that you are simply interested in what they think, most kids like sharing their ideas and opinions with their parents this way. At the same time, they will hear your opinions without having it sounding like a lecture. It can be fun to "open some of those communication doors" and when you are comfortable talking with each other in this way, it will certainly be easier to keep them open.

Through safe and respectful dialogue, each of you will practice talking with and really listening to one another. You will get to know each other better, the basis for an improved relationship. This is the goal.

If you or your child would like to let us know how What I Wish You Knew Conversations works for you, or if you have ideas about topics to include in our next book of Starters, we'd love to hear from you. Email Sharon at whatiwishyouknew@gmail.com

Starters

Below are some of the questions (Starters) that elicited the heartfelt comments in this book. Try asking one to your own child and see where the conversation takes you.

But first, be sure to read the instructions in "How to Use This Book." Pay special attention to "Don't interrupt. Listen with patience and respect. Be as courteous as you would to someone you don't love."

Students were invited to respond to some of the subjects presented below. I call these Starters. Or they could write about any topic that was of interest to them. Responses could be as long or short as they wanted. You will see pieces in the chapters that follow that are only one sentence and some that are several pages long. The kids were reminded that this was not a test or term paper. There were no wrong answers, no grades, no competition.

They were promised that their names would not be used so there was no fear of embarrassment. Knowing they had the opportunity to write anonymously, many of them poured their hearts out once they got started. If they wanted to show or talk about what they wrote with their parents or anyone else, fine. But that choice would be theirs.

As students (high school, junior high and college), they were comfortable writing to an assignment, rather than just diving in on a black piece of paper or computer screen. That was the reason I created Starters, specifically worded open-ended questions, not unlike the verbal equivalent of a Rorschach test.

Here are some of the topics and questions students and I agreed were good ones for parents and teens to use to open a discussion. Ideally, both generations will respond to issues that interest them. One suggestion for an easy "start" is for the teen to interview the parent, using the questions. Or talk about what subjects are missing and should have been included.

Our 20 questions are presented in no particular order. Any one of them might be a good Starter for a conversation in your family.

1. Advice to parents.
   What makes a good parent? Do you think people should have to take a course in parenting when they have a child? What advice would you like to give to parents or any other adult?

2. Life then and now.
   How do you think life has changed since your parents were growing up? Which generation had it easier?

3. Stress. What are some of the biggest sources of stress for kids growing up today? For adults?

4. Listening.
   How important is it? Is there someone you wish would tune in and listen to you? Is there someone you wish you didn't have to listen to?

5. Violence.
   What do you think about violence in movies and on tv? Ok or too much? Do you think that hearing about violence does any harm? Or no?

6. Body image.
   Spain's government banned models considered "too skinny," saying they wanted to set a healthier body image for young girls. What do you think of this?

7. Bullying.
   Do you know anyone who has ever been the victim or a bully? What should they do?

   What about observers? What should someone do if they see or know what is going on?

   What should happen to the bully?

   What is cyberbullying? Why is it in the news so much lately? What harm can it do?

8. Sex.
   What do parents NOT know? What SHOULD parents or other adults be aware of? Why?

9. Drinking
   Is it true that kids are drinking more now than ever before?

10. School.
    When you hear the word, "school," what is the first thing you think of?

    Is all the work at school worth it?

    If you could change the curriculum, what courses would you add? Eliminate?

11. The future.
    Do worries about the future affect your life?

12. Illness.
    Do you know anyone whose life has been touched by physical or mental illness?

13. Grief.
    Have you experienced the death of someone close to you?

14. Hopes and dreams.
   Ask your parent/child about their hopes and dreams, about
   choices they feel they do or don't have in their lives.

   If they could make five wishes, what would they be?

15. Birth order.
   Does being the older or younger one make any difference?
   What about being in the middle?

16. Influence.
   Who has been an important influence in your life? Why?
   What is the best or worst thing you learned from them?

17. Nutrition.
   Do you think that what we eat and where it comes from is
   important?

18. The environment,
   Can one person really make a difference?

19. Advice to younger kids.
    If you could give some advice to a younger brother or sister,
    or a younger child or teen anywhere in the world, what would
    you tell them?

20. Thank you.
    Is there someone in your life who deserves a thank you note?
    Even just an email or text?

This book consists of teens' responses to some of these questions in the form of letters to their parents, poems and powerful short quotes.

THEY ARE PRESENTED ANONYMOUSLY, NOT ONLY TO RESPECT THE PRIVACY OF THE WRITERS, BUT ALSO SO THAT PARENTS MIGHT WONDER IF PERHAPS ONE OF THE REMARKS THEY READ MIGHT HAVE BEEN WRITTEN BY THEIR OWN CHILD.

Thank you to the students who participated in the creation of this book. Because of you, maybe there will be one less parent asking, "How do I get my children to talk to me?"

To parents who would like to know more about what their kids think and feel, as a mother, teacher and social worker, I join you in knowing that we have much to learn from our children.

In the hope of fostering better communication between generations, with their permission, I share their words with you.

Sharon Weingarten

The Stress of Growing Up in 21st Century

What are the biggest sources of stress for kids growing up today?
Which generation had it easier, yours or your parents'?

Students were asked to say a little about what causes them
stress and what might help. Or they could choose to respond to
the question, "Which generation had an easier time growing
up, theirs or their parent's. These topics really struck a chord.
They wrote about pressures in school, at home and with peers.
They wrote about trying to live up to the expectations of parents
and of the media and how times have changed. They spoke
about very real fears they have in their "not so kiddie" childhood.

They try to help adults understand that, in order to help them
cope with their stresses, we must first be aware of them.

66*Maybe parents trivialize our problems because they don't even
know what they are.*"

Letting our children know that we are there for them and really
do want to know more about their lives might prevent small
problems from becoming big ones.

Stress

Mariana Glusman, MD

There are different ways to think about stress. The most common refers to that overwhelmed, paralyzed feeling that you get when there is too much going on, when the expectations are too much, or the consequences too high. For many teens this may mean too many extracurricular activities, unachievable social/physical expectations, and overwhelming academic competition. Piled on top of that is the worry that many teens experience at home (divorce, financial instability, domestic violence), in school (bullying, social isolation) and in their communities (gun violence, school shootings…). Add one more layer of teens' emerging awareness of world events, the environment and their uncertain future and you get a pressure cooker, ready to explode. And yet, most kids don't. Most teens adapt and adjust and keep going and you wouldn't know that they are stressed…except that they may not be sleeping or eating well, or they may seem distant and non-communicative. However, for some teens the stress turns to anxiety and depression, or illicit drug use—and for a small number to violence toward themselves (cutting, suicide) or others.

Another way to think about stress is to look at the underlying physical response to all these internal and external pressures. The "stress response" is what the body does in response to fear, whether it is internal, such as fear of failure, disappointment, loss, or external such as fear of violence or economic instability. It is also called the "fight or flight response," and is at the core of our survival as a species. Here is the way it works:

When you are exposed to a stressor, say a mountain lion about to attack, or a bully coming down the hall, the first thing that happens is the adrenal glands and parts of the brain secrete epinephrine (also known as adrenaline) and norepinephrine. These substances make your heart speed up so that more blood goes to your muscles and brain, they make your breathing faster so you pick up more oxygen, and they divert blood away from your internal organs and your skin. That's why when you are stressed you look pale. Your body also responds to stress by producing a hormone called cortisol. Cortisol is made in the adrenal glands, located just above your kidneys. Cortisol is called the stress hormone because it is needed to regulate the body's response to stress, including the production of glucose, heightened memory and attention, and lower sensitivity to pain. It is also an important part of the immune system. Without enough cortisol your body cannot fight infections well. On the other hand too much cortisol causes high blood pressure, fatigue, depression, moodiness, and weight gain as well as a decreased immune and inflammatory response. So, bottom line, stress affects cortisol, which, in turn, affects the immune system, which is responsible for our ability to fight against infectious agents and cancer. In other words—stress can make you sick.

A more recent and worrisome new finding in multiple studies, is that sustained high levels of stress without adequate support, also referred to as "toxic stress", can actually change the structure of children's brains. Even more scary, it can change the very make up of their DNA! That means that stressful events in childhood can have lifelong consequences, and may even be passed on to the next generation! The emerging field of epigenetics, which looks at the environment's effects on the genes, is sounding the warning: what we do now, will not only affect our health, but also the health of our children and their children after that... The good news is that the effects of toxic stress can be prevented and even reversed in a caring and supportive environment.

We can also talk about the stress in our society, the intense competition and accelerated expectations. Kids need to get in the right preschool to get into the right elementary school to get into the best college.... Companies like "Baby Einstein" tap into parents' fears--promoting products to help babies learn faster. Another company has a 10 DVD set for $130 with programming aimed at teaching reading skills to infants as young as 9 months to get kids ready for preschool! What is the rush? Who are we competing against? What are the consequences on our children?

The pressure to go to college and to succeed academically, while at the same time removing other outlets (like recess!) has also likely contributed to the recent ADHD epidemic. According to a recent study one in five high-school boys and one in eleven high-school girls were diagnosed with ADHD in 2011-12. Kids who are not able to stay focused for long periods of time, in crowded classrooms full of distractions, are labeled as abnormal and started on medications. In the past 8 years the number of kids and teens on ADHD drugs like Ritalin and Adderall increased by one million! What if it's not the kids, but the system that has the problem? Who is benefiting? The drug companies? The testing companies? Colleges? It is certainly not the kids.

What to do about all this stress? The first and most important step is to recognize it and to talk about it. What is causing the stress? Is it internal or external? Are the expectations appropriate and manageable? Or are they just too much? What would happen if the expectations were not met? What is the worse case scenario? What activities can be trimmed from a too busy schedule? Where can you find help? A counselor, a teacher, a doctor, a coach?

Remember that adequate support from a caring adult is what keeps high levels of stress from becoming toxic. Spending positive time together is what builds the trust that will be the scaffold for this support. We invite you to spend some time thinking and talking about stress with your teen. Sometimes being asked about stress can cause stress. What is the right answer? Will admitting to being stressed make my parents worry or be disappointed? Will it get them "off my back" or will it do the opposite? Will it be embarrassing? Will I look dumb or weak? People need to feel safe to talk about personal things. It is hard as a parent not to give advice when you hear your teen is having difficulties. It's hard not to immediately voice an opinion, or to jump in to try to help. But that is not what they need. That is not to say that they should not hear your opinions. It's a matter of timing. Being a parent is hard. Parenting a teen can be agonizing especially when things are not going well. This is why it is important to develop a relationship that focuses on the importance of open and frequent communication.

Not so kiddie childhood of today

"You ask which generation had it easier, our parents' or ours. I think theirs, for sure. Times have changed a lot since our parents were kids. Some adults pay very little attention to life in the "not so kiddie" childhood of today. It's pretty obvious that stress is more common now than in the past generations because there are lots more things to be stressed about. Growing up these days is a lot tougher than most people think. The problem isn't that some parents forget what it's like to be a kid; it is that they don't realize how fast times are changing and they make the mistake of trivializing our problems. We are immersed in a culture that parents don't understand. Sure, we may seem moody, but we have a lot on our minds."

I pretend not to care

"Society puts so much pressure on kids. Teenagers feel like they have to look or act a certain way to fit in. Nowhere in commercials do they show a fat or average person. They do the total opposite. Everyone looks perfect. Wear these jeans and those boots. Be sexy - but be a good girl and don't have sex. Be really, really thin - but don't get anorexic. Go out to eat with your friends - but don't eat the supersize portions they have in every restaurant. I know kids who actually throw up on purpose because they are scared they will gain an ounce.

I wish you knew what it feels like to go to my school, see everyone wearing the right clothes, driving the right car, and worrying about their make-up all before 8:00 a.m. They looked like they stepped right out of a magazine. I wish adults could understand what it's like to have to see this all the time and pretend not to care. I wish you could take all the labels off clothes. Let us all look more natural.

I actually wish we had school uniforms. That would cut down on a lot of pressure. You wouldn't have to worry about wearing the right clothes and about looking unpopular.

I also would have seminars at school to talk to kids about this stuff.

There should be classes about body image. These classes should talk about ways to handle pressure too. And adults should have to take them also.

I don't believe they even had school shootings then.

" *We read the papers and watch T.V. How can you not be stressed? Our parent's generation definitely had it easier. I don't believe they even had school shootings then.*

How can you not be stressed when you're scared to death most of the time? When they were kids they didn't have to worry so much about being kidnapped. Or raped or shot. Now it's dangerous to walk home from a friend's house. Or take a bus. Or just go to school or go shopping or a movie in Colorado or Utah or Virginia or Wisconsin or Connecticut or Chicago or Minnesota or Florida or Texas or South Carolina, Florida again.

We shouldn't have to live like this, we shouldn't have to die like this.

I sure hope that high school is not the best time of my life.

"My parents have said, 'What stress could you possibly have? You are a child whose only responsibility is to go to school. 'These are the best years of your life.'

I sure hope that high school is not the best time of my life. Stress is everywhere and in everything. This century is developing very fast, but my stress isn't from the technology, it is mainly from things that happen in school. High school is so nerve racking that I wish parents could relive what it's like to go through this, starting right from kindergarten."

Much easier for their generation.

"*Growing up these days is harder than most adults think. Now, more than ever, teenagers are held to the highest expectations, much more than I think my parents ever faced. My father told me his college application process consisted of his going to the college counselor at his high school, writing an essay, and going out there and making his parents proud. What a joke! High school students today are taking classes that most adults took when they were in college. School is much more difficult now. Plus, with all the new discoveries in science and technology, more knowledge is being forced on us to prepare us for work in the real world.*

And all the homework! Is there really a need for this much homework? Sometimes I feel so overworked in school that I feel like I'm going to go crazy."

It's like we are never good enough to be who we really are.

❝ *We are constantly being pressured to compete. My life is filled with other people's expectations of me to be the best... the best student, the best athlete, the wonderful daughter, the good friend. Then their expectations become my own. I feel like I am never good enough.*

An American teenage lifestyle seems idealistic, but growing up in modern day American society is no joy ride. Pressure is everywhere, and as the pressure rises, so does the stress. Whether it is peer, parent, or even just the pressure we put on ourselves, it has a major impact. Every kid is trying to reach higher and higher expectations, like thinking you should be the class valedictorian, the star of the basketball team, or fitting into a size zero pair of jeans. How did the standard go from trying your best to being (what someone thinks is) perfect? ❞

A big source of stress is parents, telling us we can do anything when, in reality, we know we can't.

" *Flawless performance is always expected. It seems that it is never good enough for us to be who we really are. We are constantly being pressured to do more and be the best, and pressure like this can really set us off.*

I feel like if I were a mountain, my parents would expect me to be at the top so I could rule it. It's like I'm supposed to rush to become the president of the world or the scientist who discovers a cure for cancer.

There is no room for "just hanging out" time anymore, because every moment of the day is so focused on reaching goals and meeting their expectations. There's no time to just chill. My parents think that every minute I need to be doing something. Don't be late for work, did you call Grandma, your room is a mess, homework comes before anything, if you want to use the car you have to pick up your little sister from her friend's house, did you write the thank you notes, you need to rewrite that essay so you can at least try to get into a good college, don't do drugs, hurry or you'll never get to work on time.

I can't breathe!

Our school day is just as overwhelming and exhausting as their workday.

"I think that parents don't understand that our school day is just as overwhelming and exhausting as their workday, and our lives can be just as stressful as theirs is for them. Kids don't have experience with so many commitments and we don't know where to turn first. I wish adults understood how overwhelming all this can be for us. Pressures and stress can get really bad when you're trying to fit everything together perfectly – school, sports, homework, family, friends, work. You try your best but there is continuous pressure. There is no way you can excel in everything.

And some of us have more than schoolwork on our minds. We have additional stress from relationships, and other things parents probably don't have a clue about."

How Can We Reduce Our Stress?

Written by 17 year old student

❝*There is no teenager on the planet, who, if given the opportunity, would not choose to lead a stress-free life. We all wish we lived in a Utopian society where stress was some evil known only in fictional stories. Unfortunately, this is not the case, and stress is a part of everyday life. Luckily for America's youth, however, there are several methods whereby an individual's stress level can be greatly reduced.*

Method One: Parents need to layoff.

Granted, during the teenage years especially, parents must have a significant role in the lives of their children, but there is a line that needs to be drawn. Every day, just as parents go to work to earn money, children go to school, ideally to learn. Consequently, just as parents sometimes need "special treatment" after a particularly difficult day at the office, children should be granted the same privilege. We work hard too, and while we know that we also have household responsibilities, it would be nice if parents understood that we have days where we are stressed, and they adjusted their actions towards us accordingly. This could serve to greatly alleviate already mounting stress.

Method Two: Teachers should be more understanding.

The average students needs (ideally) 8 hours of sleep, attends 7 hours of school, and in the case of many of America's youth, participates in 2-6 hours of work and/or extracurricular activities. Usually, this leaves time for several hours of homework. However, on days where the stress level is high (i.e. a big exam, project, or extracurricular event), it would be nice if teachers understood that students may need an extra day to complete an assignment. Such a small action could go a long way in lessening a student's stress.

Method Three: Kids need to relax.

There is absolutely nothing wrong with taking a break from homework to watch some TV, get a snack, or chat with a friend. Parents should understand this fact and let their child be. However, one must make sure that the break does not last too long, or if may be after midnight before the homework is finished. And sleeping less will certainly not reduce stress.

Though stress is not a pleasant part of any teenager's life, it is a necessary evil. Some stress can even be good, especially when it motivates a student to do better work.

Stress is not, however, something that should be ignored. Every person in a teenager's life has the ability to lessen his stress load: parents, teachers, and friends. We don't ask you to make sure that we have no stress; all we ask is that you try to help us deal with it."

Advice to Parents and Other Adults

What would you like to tell parents and other adults?

Most of the students I interviewed felt that adults don't appreciate how much times have changed in recent years. They strongly feel that even the most well-intentioned parents have a lot to learn. They welcomed the opportunity to offer advice to parents and schools and adults in general, but mainly to parents.

66 *Parents assume that teaching good values can protect their children from making bad choices. They think, 'My kid gets good grades, doesn't do drugs and gets home by curfew so I'm a good parent.'*

Wrong!"

Wanting to help adults be better parents was a theme that was repeated often. They felt that the most important thing parents should learn is to be better listeners.

66 *Please take some time out of your busy, busy lives to just listen to what we have to say."*

Another issue most adults will readily recognize is the fact that teens often contradict themselves. They know it! Read what these students have to say.

We crave independence, but...

"We crave independence but still, deep down, we want our parents to take care of us. We just don't want to have parents in our face all the time.

Teenagers are hard to talk to and we know it. Just the same, though, we need parents to hear our worries about friends and grades and to understand our fears about school, finding a job, everything.

As much as we contradict ourselves and switch rapidly between wanting our parents to baby us and protect us – and pushing them out of our lives – in the end we just want a safety net, someone to back us up. We want to feel that someone who wants the best for us is there and willing to just sit and listen."

Be tuned in, but also have your own life

I need you
to know who I am
to accept me as I change and grow
to be aware of what my life is like
to be a good observer
to be a good listener
and
to have your own life.

Don't take everything so personally

Mom, I know I give you a hard time, but sometimes I can't help it. My advice to you is not to take it so personally. Just let me be and know it's not really about you. I know I don't always act like it, but I really do love you.

p.s.
I'm glad I can write anonymously because I would never say this out loud."

You're in a hard place, but so are we

*Dear Parents,*

We ask the impossible. I am 17 years old and I realize this. You're in a hard place, but so are we. We want parents and adults to be available at all times to listen to us about whatever we feel like talking about.

We also want you to leave us alone if we come home exhausted and not in the mood to talk and just want to be alone. We want you to give us advice if you have it, but we really want to just be acknowledged, listened to and comforted and told that a solution will come and that we will be capable of carrying it out.

Teenagers realize that part of growing up is doing lots of things along the way that later don't seem quite so wise or praiseworthy. We need parents and adults to listen, to hear about our actions and our reasoning. We need you to realize that we're still learning things as we go along, and that, unfortunately, the best way to learn the right way to do things is to do them the wrong way, sometimes even more than once. Don't judge us or make us feel guilty all the time. Just listen to us.

Don't scare us off by hearing our worries and running off half-cocked to try to fix them. Sometimes we don't even want action; we just want to be able to rant. Adults have learned how important it is to have a close friend or more experienced person to vent to, bounce ideas off of and receive advice from. Adults choose a support network of people who listen, accept and don't judge. That's who they should be for their kids. We need someone to listen to us and hear our worries without feeling the need to always be imparting wisdom."

Especially when we are going through hard times

The following is a portion of an essay from a 16 year old student

Teens are sometimes not able to express themselves easily. Some kids deal with anorexia, bulimia, trying to look good, not being too fat, not being too thin, pressure from friends, fear of having no friends, being told we have the wrong friends.

Sometimes when parents observe troubling behaviors in their children they lose their common sense in attempts to help. They will buy an expensive gift or take them on a luxury trip, hoping it will show their child how much they are loved. Some will send their child off to camp for the summer so when they return they will be 'fixed.' By doing things like this the most reasonable solutions and steps to recovery will have been overlooked.

One of the hardest, but simplest things a parent can do is listen, especially when your teen is going through hard times. If the child is harming herself, being able to talk with you might help her make the first step toward recovery. Through that process the parents and teens will uncover things that maybe led to the destructive behavior. The process of finding the source and dealing with it will not be fast or simple, but at the end the family will be left with closeness and a positive outlook for times ahead.

Listening is not a parent's first instinct or idea on how to help their teen, but it truly will reap the most benefits in the long run. By talking less and listening more, parents will have a better understanding of what their child is going through. When they are listening instead of talking it makes it easier for us to approach them with problems.

Even if your teen does not want to talk, just being there and sitting with us can be comforting. The presence of someone who cares is the best treatment for a vulnerable or emotionally unstable teen. In a time filled with loneliness someone with an open mind and open ears is the most needed."

"Act your age. *Parents should not try to be in our group. You are not one of our friends. Don't start acting like you like the same music we like or wearing the same clothes because it is just embarrassing."*

"Don't make your kids afraid to tell you their problems. *Growing up involves making a lot of decisions we later recognize are not examples of our finest thinking. But we can't learn anything if we are constantly terrified of making a mistake or of letting you down. It makes me afraid to tell you when I have a problem. Just try to sympathize with what I'm dealing with.*

"Parents should try to stay involved even if we say we don't want you to, no matter what. *Talk to us. Know who we are. Ask about what's going on, anything. Ask about our friends even if you don't like them."*

❝My advice to parents? Be honest. If you don't know the an-swer, say so. *I know you aren't perfect and I don't expect you to be, but I can tell when you are making up things and all that does is make me stop asking you anything."*

❝Don't wait till your child gets pregnant or is arrested. *Some kids want to be able to sit down and talk to their parents about important things but many adults shut their teens out until it is shoved in their faces.*

Some parents do a better job than others of knowing what their children want and need at certain points in their lives. Some are better parents when their children are babies."

❝TEENS NEED A GUIDE, NOT A GUARD."

"Don't talk too much and don't always be teaching.
Sometimes you can be so totally annoying that the only thing I can do is just tune you out. You talk too much. My advice to you is not to talk so much. Maybe then I would listen to you more.

If parents want to have a conversation with their kids, do it, but don't try to make everything into an issue. Don't criticize us about how we feel. And don't always be trying to fix us with your advice. Don't always be pointing the way. Don't always be teaching. "

"Stop screaming at me. Yelling does not get your point across. My advice is to pay attention to what works and what doesn't. Screaming at me just makes me tune you out more. "

"The key is encouragement, not criticism. Parents should be patient. Don't put us down for everything we do wrong, but praise us for what we do right. Just that little thing will make a lot of difference. It would make me try harder the next time. Instead of always hassling us, cut us some slack. Help us out instead of always being so hard on us.

You don't need to yell at me because inside I punish myself every time I screw up, which is most of the time. "

"Too much support is not good. *Sometimes too much of a good thing is too much. Most parents don't realize that all their support can lead to anxiety. Give me some space and stop pushing so hard. If I get 95 on a test you ask me why not 100? I want to enjoy my life and not live for some imaginary future ideal that can never be reached. Everyone is pushing kids, especially our own parents. I know you guys mean well but too much of your 'help for our own good' is not so helpful. What you call support just causes me anxiety. No, I cannot do anything I set my mind to!"*

"Don't only be interested in my school work. Take an interest in all of my life, not only be so worried about my school work. *It seems that is all you care about. Pay attention to what is happening in my life NOW, more than what I will be in the future."*

"Don't always be trying to protect me so much. *Just be understanding when I have problems and try to help me out if I need you to."*

❝ *Some parents should control their kids for their own good.*

There are things parents don't have a clue about. "

❝ *I need you to be the parent so I can be the kid.* *It scares me when you always tell me to use my own judgment. We don't like to admit it, but we really need you to act like parents. Someone needs to be in charge. I need you to be the parent so I can be the kid.*

You should be a good role model. Don't tell me not to do something when you're the one I learned it from. If you don't want your kids to drink like you do, don't always be drinking. If you don't want your kids to smoke and drink and swear like you do, don't always be smoking and drinking and swearing. "

Some comments by some high school freshmen and middle school students worthy of discussion

"*One question was about if kids are drinking and using drugs more now than ever before.* My answer is YES. I see a lot of kids doing stuff in really young grades. Parents should know that.

And peers have a major effect on each other. If you don't join them in drinking or doing drugs, how will they react? Will they still be your friends?

"*People wonder how teens get their hands on drugs.* At my school it's about as hard as borrowing a pencil."

"*Our society sends contradictory messages.* Turn on the TV. All day you hear about buying drugs to help you deal with your problems."

"*If a friend does it, it can't be that bad, can it?*"

What's a Parent to Do?

Kate Mahoney, MSW, LCSW

"While most teens choose not to use alcohol or other drugs, every teen will be faced with making decisions about mood-alerting substances. Teens are faced with making these decisions over and over again. Alcohol and other drugs are widely available to teens as part of their environment. Whether or not they are available in your home, alcohol and prescription medications are widely accessible in many homes in local communities. I have had countless teens recount stories of unsupervised drinking parties and "pharming parties" that they have attended at the homes of neighbors and friends. "Pharming parties" involve raiding medicine cabinets for prescription and over-the-counter medications, sometimes mixing them with alcohol, sometimes not. It should also be noted that "unsupervised parties" can take place when parents are home, if they agree to be banished to another floor of the home, or if parents drink or get high while a group of teens gathers at their home.

Teens today experience a great deal of stress. Many teens have wonderful opportunities and are highly accomplished scholars, athletes, musicians and writers. Many teens are very generous with their time and make significant contributions through their outstanding community service. Many of those same teens are at great risk for substance abuse and other problems. I have worked with team captains, straight A students, student government leaders and other wonderful teens, who turn to alcohol and other drugs to numb themselves from pain, to make them thin, to keep their energy up so that they can continue to excel, or to create an image that they think will meet the expectations of others. A lot of teens are really hurting inside, and yet often the people who love them the most...their parents, don't see the depth of the pain, fear, anxiety or drug use.

There are many things parents can do to help their teens navigate the challenges of adolescence. Be clear about your expectations that your child should not drink until at least age 21, when it is legal to do so. Remind your child not to use other people's medications and that you still want to know what over-the-counter medications and supplements they are taking. Most importantly, keep the lines of communication open. Keep talking even when you don't get the reply you might want. Keep listening. Keep telling your children that you love them, even when they ask you to drop them off a block from school when it is pouring rain and you know that they would rather get drenched than be seen being dropped off by their parent.

I know this sounds like quite a tall order. It is. Parenting teens may perhaps be one of the hardest things you will ever do in your life. I know that it will be one of the most rewarding. Nurture yourself along the way. Get support. Also talk to other parents. You are not the only one who is trying to set limits and navigate the difficult balance of trust, accountability and safety."

"*Keep encouraging your kids.*

The teen years are probably the worst for any parent and mine would probably agree, but my folks were pretty cool. They trusted me and always encouraged me to try new things and let me know they had confidence in me. Sometimes all that cheerleading was pretty annoying, but as I look back now I have to say I really appreciate it.

More advice from children and teens

❝Treat me as well as you do your friends. *Actually, you should pay more attention to your kids than your friends.*

❝ *Don't take out your problems on your kids.*

❝Don't talk about me like I am not even in the room. *You should show me some respect too.*

❝Don't spoil me. *I know that I should not have everything I ask for.*

❝ *Don't correct me in front of people.*

❝ *Don't worry about the number of hours we spend together.* *It's about how it feels when we are together that counts, not all that time when I can tell you are so distracted and thinking about work – or anything but me.*

❝ *Don't be inconsistent.* *That makes me try harder to get away with everything I can. It also makes me know you aren't sure about things yourself.*

❝ *Don't make promises you can't keep.*

❝ *Be proud of me.*

❝ *Don't do things for me that I can do for myself.*

"Don't scare me with your threats. *I end up telling lies and digging myself into a hole I can't climb out of.*

"Give me some space. *Don't "helicopter" and always be hovering.*

"Don't cut me off when I do talk to you.

"Let kids be kids. *Give me some space and don't push so hard. I need space to breathe.*

"Realize that it is not the end of the world to make a mistake or be human.

"All teenagers need is to be recognized, loved and respected.

"We are not babies anymore. *I hate when adults talk to me in that condescending tone.*

" *Apologize when you are wrong.*

" *Listen to me when I want to talk*

" **Don't just ask me questions.** *Talk to me too. Communication should be a two-way street. I wish parents would share more about their lives.*

" **Parents should have a good memory.** *You were a kid once.*

" **Be prepared.** *I am only a freshman in high school, but I can tell you parents, if you have young children, be prepared because when those teen years come around, it's going to be hard on you. There is no foolproof guide to parenting, but try your best.*

Some advice for schools

66 *Bring your parents to school day. How can parents understand what they don't know? I think it would be great if schools offered classes where parents could learn how kids spend their days. Maybe if they had a Bring Your Parents to School Day every week or every month people could get some insight. If they understood more about our lives, we'd have more to talk about instead of just always saying, how was school.*

66 *Schools should provide programs for teachers and parents and let kids talk. Then they should listen to the advice that kids offer. Maybe parents and teachers too, could learn to understand more. Parents and teens could start to settle some things."*

66 *My idea to help with the overwhelming amount of homework is that teachers should work together and plan to give heavy homework loads and tests on separate days. They should have meetings in which they plan out tests and projects for the week. Every subject should have a test day, like math tests on Mondays and all language tests on Tuesdays, etc. That would help."*

66 *There should be a time management class in high schools."*

The American Academy of Pediatrics declared the chronic sleepiness of our nation's teenagers a public health issue. And to help fix the problem, the organization called for middle and high schools to push back their start times 30 to 60 minutes to allow students to get more rest.

"A substantial body of research has now demonstrated that delaying school start times is an effective countermeasure to chronic sleep loss," the organization said. "The American Academy of Pediatrics strongly supports the efforts of school districts to optimize sleep in students."

Sleep deprivation in teenagers is widespread. Eighty-seven percent of high school students in the U.S. are getting less than the recommended 8.5 to 9.5 hours of sleep, and high school seniors get less than 7 hours of sleep a night, on average, the AAP says. In addition, 28 percent of high school students report falling asleep at school at least once a week, while 1 in 5 say they fall asleep doing homework with similar frequency.

The exhaustion has serious consequences. The American Academy of Pediatrics reports that the average teenager in the U.S. regularly experiences levels of sleepiness similar to people with sleep disorders such as narcolepsy. Adolescents are also at higher risk for car accidents resulting from drowsy driving. And lack of sleep affects mood, attention, memory and behavior control.

So can't they just go to bed earlier? Studies suggest that at the onset of adolescence, there is a delay in when the body starts to secrete melatonin, a hormone that tells the body it's time to go to sleep. Researchers have also found that it takes the adolescent brain longer to wind down and fall asleep after being awake for 14.5 to 18.5 hours than it does for people in other stages of life. According to the American Academy of Pediatrics, "this research indicates that the average teenager in today's society has difficulty falling asleep before 11 p.m. and is best suited to wake up at 8 a.m. or later."

"I wish my school knew that the adolescent sleep cycle involves not getting up so early. I wish they realized that there are actual physical reasons I need to sleep late."

Schools should teach about the effects of harassment.

High school can be vicious. *"We need classes in high school that teach the importance of respecting a person's individuality. People underestimate some of the things that we go through, things that might seem invisible to the adult naked eye. For all the teachers and parents out there, do not think it is so easy being a teen in today's world. We have things to worry about. Teachers and parents don't realize the tormenting that goes on in school. Some of us can't even walk down the hall without looking behind our back. When someone is being bullied, they can feel like they have no place on earth."*

I wish teachers could be the students for a day. *Maybe then they will really know what we go through. I think they don't realize the amount of teasing and tormenting that goes on when no one is looking. What happens in school really makes a difference. We spend more time there than at home and the effect a teacher can have is huge. They get degrees in the subjects they teach, but some don't seem to know much about kids. They can cause embarrassment and make things worse."*

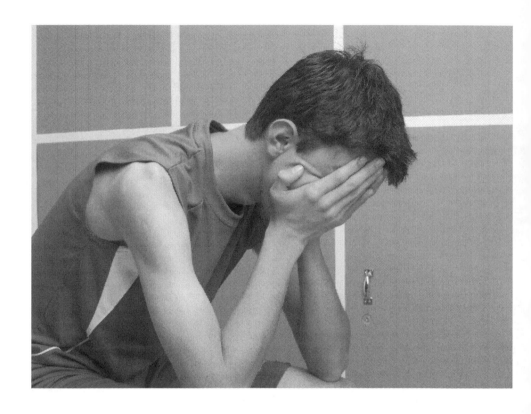

If everybody had to go...

"*Even though someone might look cool as a cucumber on the outside, you never know what they are going through in their minds.* *Sometimes kids aren't sure of what to do about their problems and as the days go by, it all just gets worse. A lot of thoughts and emotion get smashed together.*

I don't' say anything to anyone and just hope things will get better. Some days I just wish I could disappear.

Maybe if all students had to meet with the social worker or school counselor on a regular basis, it could help. And if everybody had to do it, it wouldn't be like somebody had problems or anything."

When to worry

The decision to seek professional help for your child can be difficult. All children experience problems on their way to becoming adults. They may have difficulty coping, feel sad and moody or become involved with alcohol or drugs. The decision to seek professional help should be based on the intensity and duration of the problem. Is it interfering with his day to day functioning?

If you observe emotional or behavioral problems over a period of time, it is wise to consult with a professional.

Seek <u>immediate</u> professional evaluation if your child exhibits

- Behaviors that pose a danger to others or involve intentional violence toward people or animals

- Expressions of suicidal ideation, threats of self-harm or harm to others

Keep in mind <u>duration</u> and <u>intensity</u> of the following symptoms:

- Behavior problems at school, requiring intervention

- Incidents requiring police intervention such as vandalism and theft

- Marked decline in school performance

- Frequent truancy

- Sexual acting out

- Repeated use of alcohol and or drugs

- Persistent, sustained and prolonged negative mood, including loss of pleasure in previously enjoyed activities, withdrawing from people and activities, "shutting down"

- Increased somatic complaints, such as stomachaches or headaches without medical basis

- Marked change in eating habits, sudden weight gain or excessive dieting, including throwing up or using laxatives to lose weight

- Persistent sleep problems such as insomnia, nightmares- or wanting to sleep all the time

- Frequent outbursts of anger at people and situations

- Frequent episodes of crying and/or expressions of hope-lessness

- Repeated threats to run away

Contact Mental Health America www.mentalhealthamerica.net. 800-969-NMHA(6642) for a referral to specific mental health service or support program in your community.

A Glimpse into the Diaries of Teens

It has been my privilege to communicate with teens from around the world, to be allowed into their lives and hear some of their stories, their dreams, wishes, joys, frustrations and fears.

Students were invited to share anything they wanted to be included in this collective journal of teen voices. In all honesty, I was surprised that so many wanted to submit entries, but they did! They wrote in the form of essays, poems, letters to parents, whatever they liked. The difference between this chapter and the ones that precede it is the fact that, for this one, the kids were not asked to write to a specific topic, such as Stress or Advice. This was open to them to write whatever they liked.

A Glimpse into the Diaries of Teens is a compilation of what they had to say. They are just literal glimpses into what might be diary entries. The purpose of sharing them is consistent with earlier chapters, hoping that there might be one less family saying, "If only we had known what was in his head..."

The writings that follow are purposefully presented in no particular order, although we did try to group similar subjects together. They are simply thoughts, feelings and opinions that teens wanted to express, to get off their chests and were willing to share. The writers ask only that adults read what they have to say with respect.

Thank you to the many students who wrote. What you had to say might just help somebody else's parents have some newfound empathy for their own child.

In addition to being a good way for the kids to "vent," this is a great opportunity for adults to have more good talking points or STARTERS for conversations with their own teens.

As a parent myself, some of these writings made me feel like crying, some like smiling. Parents, share your reaction to reading the entries in this chapter with your child. Remember, it is easier to talk about someone else's experiences and feelings than our own. But first, re-read **How to Use this Book.**

**Dear Parents,**

Some days you make me not want to come home. *What I wish you knew is that our lives are not as easy as you may think. Home is supposed to be the place where we are accepted and where we can find refuge from the stress of school and the whole outside world. Some days you make me not want to come home. This wears me down. Where do you want me to go?*

The fact is that I actually do try in school. It would be nice to get some credit from you, instead of your constantly putting me down for my less than perfect grades. You can't believe the competition in school. Do you think we can all get into ivy league colleges? Do you think I can?

I also wish you knew about those "friends" of mine that you like so much. You have no idea of the pressure they give me to do certain things that I think you wouldn't like so much. Kids these days are faced with an ever-increasing amount of tough choices and decisions. It is important for parents to be more nurturing and supportive. The increase in teens' risky behavior is not just due to chance. Don't make me not want to come home.

**Dear Mom and Dad,**

I wish you knew you don't know how to handle me. *I'm a really good kid. I get good grades. I work hard. I'm involved in extracurricular activities. I'm class president. I don't drink or party or smoke. I've been with my boyfriend for a year and a half, and we're not having sex. I make good life choices. And a lot of that comes from you.*

The thing is, I can't talk to you guys. You're so set in your ways, your opinions are so small, you gossip and hate people because of the way you were raised, and I can't stand it.

When my boyfriend and I get in fights over things I can't even come to you, because you don't like him and you don't want us to be together, and I'm scared every time I ask you if I can see him. (Which is ridiculous because he's such a good kid. He'll probably be valedictorian. He's one of the only normal people I know who doesn't drink or get high on a weekly basis. He's so respectful, and he's driven and self-motivated and he motivates me too. How can you not want us to be together?) You don't know we spend time alone in his room, or that I want to sleep over there because he treats me like a princess and brushes the hair out of my face and hugs me tight. You don't know his mom is soo okay with me staying over, she invited me to come on vacation with them this summer. You don't know I'll probably end up staying there one night, and you'll never know.

You don't understand how hard I work. That I don't just go to school from 8 to 5, but I do homework until 11. That I'm up once a week until 1:30 working on the newspaper- that I created. That I get burnt out.

I know when daddy comes home from work he's allowed to be exhausted and just want to eat and crawl into bed. I know daddy works really hard but so do I. I work as hard as I possibly can and I'm exhausted.

So I'm sorry if you don't like something I wrote in my paper. I'm sorry if I forgot to read or return the form for my summer class. I'm sorry because I don't care, and you yelling at me about it just makes me dislike you.

I'm a big girl, big enough to learn from my own mistakes. I'm big enough to realize when I've made a mistake. You don't need to remind me, and if you want to make a comment I'm open to hearing it but I've got my life under control. I don't need you to rebuke me. I don't need anyone to rebuke me. It's annoying and it means you don't have faith in me or how I'm doing.

I'm sorry I haven't turned in my forms, but dammit I can hardly keep my head up. I'm exhausted, and that form came in the middle of me studying for APs. Excuse me for it not being a priority, especially because they're so casual about deadlines. Especially because I go to a school where deadlines don't apply. Especially because I'm still a kid, my full-time job is still school, and I've never had to fill out paperwork before.

So let me learn as I go, because it's the only way I will. And just so you know, I'm willing to deal with the consequences of missing that deadline (which is having to pack my own pillow instead of getting one there.) It's no big deal, it's not life or death, so leave me alone.

You thought you struck a chord by telling me to act like an adult, but you just pissed me off. Yeah, I'm becoming an adult, and I'm growing into it.

The point is I'm still 17! That's not an adult, not even legally. And I know so many adults who miss deadlines and are FINE. I'm not going to become one of those adults, I'm working on it ON MY OWN, but damn it! Leave me alone.

Letters to my mom, my step-dad and my real-dad

Dear Mom,

I know you try to be supermom, but don't; it's impossible and stresses me out because your focus is to be super and not to really care.

Dear step-dad,

I love you like my dad, but you have a one-track mind. You need to learn to listen and not react, because if not, I'm gonna keep snapping at you.

Dear real-dad,

I don't want you in my life, You make it hell and have since I was born. I mean, couldn't you have just been there instead of with another woman?

Stop promising me stuff that you're not gonna do; just leave me alone, that's all I want from you.

Sincerely, The thirteen year old that's had so much trauma she feels like thirty."

Some Things I Hope and Want

"*I hope there are no wars, no fights, no drugs, no violence.*

I hope that my family and I could find a safe life as immigrants.

I hope that every person in the world could live in peace.

I hope that every person is treated fairly, not by their skin color, but by how intelligent they are.

I hope that white people, black people, Chinese people, Indian people, Latino people could all live in peace and just be able to be together.

I hope there are no more terrorist attacks that destroy buildings and make people suffer.

I hope every child gets a chance to study and be something.

I just hope that everyone is treated fairly and could live in peace. Even animals.

My biggest dream is to be like Mahatma Ghandi, to just live in peace. The best dream for the future is that everyone should live together like Martin Luther King Jr. said.

Why do I worry so much about my dreams? I worry about my whole life. My dream is that everyone could just live in peace.

I am afraid that I am going to get killed by violence.

I am also afraid that my family and me might have to leave the country because we are immigrants.

I worry about my parents losing their jobs.

I am concerned about my future. Since there is racism in some schools, I am concerned about my education and getting a successful future. So I have apprehension about my financial life.

I see other teens that have stress joining gangs and using drugs and doing bad things, and I am worried that if I have a lot of stress I might turn out to be like them.

I have some other dreams too. I want to be a pilot and I want to spend more time with my family.

I want to study at Harvard University and graduate from there. Then I want to be the best pilot to ever drive a plane.

I want no racism.

I want to have a business so I can make money and save for my children to come.

I want to be an excellent role model for my kids.

I want to be the richest guy in the world like Bill Gates.

I want to be popular.

I want to be joyful with my family.

I want to be something in my life.

I have a lot of concerns about my life, like a lot of us do. I deal with them and I will never give up.

I am 13. No one ever asked me about things like this before.

"No one knows that I am still a virgin. (14 year old girl)

"I think maybe I'm gay. I don't know who to talk to.

"Write something about my life?
I am in high school.
High school is hell!
I can't wait to get out."

"I could never tell my parents about it, but i wish they knew
how hard it is to be a kid from another country in an Ameri-
can school some days."

❝Evereday is a challenge. *I feel like it is a challenge just to go through the day at school unnoticed and get to the safe zone of home. And is home really all that safe? Will mom, dad or my brother be arguing? Will the people I love be home from the army safely? Will my mom ever be happy?*

I hope that someday I will not have these awful feelings in the pit of my stomach, that I will feel comfortable in my own skin and I will just be happy, rather than angry at everything so much of the time. I wish being a kid was simplified, like going from point A to point B, with the total coming out to the precise answer of C.

I hope that someday I can just have things fit into place. I want friends I can talk to without feeling that they might betray me at any moment. Sometimes I feel like things are closing in – do the right thing, get the best grades, talk to the right kids, join the right clubs. Parents, teachers, everybody, why can't you just leave me alone?

Why do I have to make decisions so much younger than they did a century ago? I'm just starting high school. Back off, let me breathe.

"*I am a Latina and because I don't have a social security
number I am afraid I will never get a good paying job.** Or a
scholarship, which is the only way I can go to college. But I hope
that one day people like me will be able to have the opportunity to
realize their dreams.*

*For now, at least I know I have my family and I know they will
always be with me. If I am ever successful I want to be able to
provide for my parents. They came to the United States from
Mexico and faced many obstacles. They didn't know English
and they had money problems but, even with their difficulties,
they worked hard and they give everything to their children.
I want to give back to them one day. I have strong hopes for
the future.*

"I have it easy. *I am an average teenager who likes playing sports and hanging out with my friends and I am very lucky.*

I got accepted into a really good college and can study whatever I want. I have a great girlfriend, my own car and live in a pretty cool frat house. My parents pay for what I need and for lots of things I don't need, but just want.

I know I sound spoiled, but I don't think I am spoiled if I realize how lucky I am.

Fixated on Looks

"As a society we have become immensely fixated on our looks
and I say WE because I am not excluding myself from the generalization. However, I being a teenage girl in this society, it is seen as almost okay.

That being said, I have also succumbed to the pressure that has been forced upon us to be "perfect" or as seamlessly perfect as the newest and most improved medicines, cosmetics and chemicals we apply, swallow and inject into our bodies can make us. Now I will be completely and perfectly honest when I say this. I am not satisfied with how I look. There are those days when I feel one or more, but never all, aspects of my looks and body seem to be as close to perfect as I can make them. But then there are those days when I hate my hair or I hate my eyes or the ever popular I wish I was as skinny as some other people and yadda yadda yadda so on and so forth. So I change something, anything, to make me feel better about me.

And as soon as I feel better I think to hell with the people out there as long as I feel better about who I am. Why should it even matter to them? But as soon as I step out the door to go with my friends I am reminded by my inner doubt...will they like it? For me its one thing to not care what my enemies think about it or even just people I'm friendly with, but my FRIENDS. It's not even that I want them to like it, it's more like I need them to like it. Why is this?

Who they think I am/ Should be

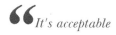*It's acceptable*

If the only thing bright about a woman is her hair,

Because really, she only has to be as clever as

The clothes she wears.

She just has to know when to show off some skin,

That is, provided, she's naturally thin,

And preferably pouty, with a voice like a child's,

Because mathematic calculations and library

Recitations are not what drive men wild.

And isn't that how she proves she's a winner?

In the number of guys who will pay for her dinner,

And how many times she picks salad as the meal,

And the way she walks away in super high heels.

Because women should have six inches, not six digits , for their figures.

They can be society's dolls.

And validate themselves though barking cat-calls,

Spend mountains of money on products and creams

To let make up and face wash

Bra cups and lip-gloss

Dominate their dreams.

It's alright if they're objectified,

They prefer it that way, it's justified.

Why else would they try so hard for a man's approval?

Or model in nothing for American Apparel?

Vs. 2
Who I really am

"*I am more than my face, my clothes, my gender,*

I'm more than some picture on a poster could render

I'm more than what only a mirror could show,

I'm more or less more than most people Know.

See, sometimes I overflow with words,

Like if books could grow wings like birds,

And fly out of me, cuz I can't keep them in.

Because underneath make-up, there's more than just skin.

Because women don't need men to give them self-worth.

They can think about more than just jewelry and child birth,

They shouldn't be embarrassed to sound clever or smart

Or to make more money than their male counterpart.

Because it's ok to be pretty,

As long as it's also ok to be witty.

I hope to be a counselor

"*I hope one day to be a counselor for girls because I know what it was like to need one and now I know what it is like to have an adult friend who accepts me and tries to help me achieve my goals.*

My story is that I am fat. Really fat, so much that even my own family makes fun of me. I have tried exercise and all kinds of diets but nothing worked. Things got so bad that I ended up having to go to the hospital. Actually, that turned out to be a good thing because the pressures from home and school were beginning to destroy me. I cried all the time and hated everyone.

There are people who think I am in the hospital because I am weak, but it is really the opposite. I am here because I am strong enough to want to get better. I am learning to take better care of myself and I am learning to trust people. That might not sound like such a big thing, but it is for me.

I am also learning that having the goal of being a perfect skinny girl is not ideal and not perfect and not healthy. They should take out all the ads in magazines and TV, glorifying only beautiful people and all the teens are slender and handsome and having sex. They should show regular or even fat kids who aren't so beautiful. It's not just me. Lots of teens are bothered by this.

Dear Mom,

"I wish you didn't worry so much about your weight. *You worry about it a lot; your mother made you worry about your appearance to an unhealthy degree when you were growing up and you always have. I used to be unhappy about my appearance, even though I'm not overweight at all. I'm a dancer and I have a very athletic body, but nevertheless, I used to be highly uncomfortable with it. This year I decided to stop worrying. I'm very stubborn and when I set my mind to something, it's hard to dissuade me from my resolution. I know this method won't work for everyone, but I decided to stop worrying about my weight and instead be confident and happy, and I was able to change my mindset just like that. The truth is, I actually have a very beautiful body. I don't believe in judging people by their looks—everyone's true beauty is inside them—but by society's standards, I am a beautiful young woman. I've been so much happier and more comfortable with myself this year; not worrying about the way I look has taken a HUGE weight off my shoulders (no pun intended...).*

So many people (particularly women) are unhappy with their appearances. I used to be one of them, but now that I've gotten over that, I want everyone to make the change that I did and stop obsessing over their body images. It took me a long time to start thinking the way I now do, but now that I've changed my outlook, I'm impatient with other people who can't make the switch I have. I'm so much happier now and I want everyone to be able to achieve the contentment and comfort level that I have.

I know that you love your kids more than anything and would never want to be overly critical of me or make me unduly uncomfortable, but you project your body image concerns onto me. You tell me I'm beautiful and I know you mean it, but you also told me that you thought a skirt I was wearing was unflattering. I'm not so much offended as I am concerned about why you said this. Everyone else (I'm not exaggerating) who has seen me wear that skirt thinks I look fantastic in it. I bought it because I thought it looked great on me. But you thought that just because it's short and I'm not as thin as a twig, it was unflattering. Eventually I told you how many compliments I've gotten on it and you accepted what I said and replied, "I stand corrected." I appreciate that; I just wish that you could feel comfortable enough about yourself to open your mind to the possibility that people who aren't sticks can have hot legs too.

After my prom, you commented that you didn't think a girl in my prom group had a very flattering dress. She's a big girl and the dress was fairly short. I thought it looked really good on her and I told you so. I didn't only want to defend her; I genuinely thought it was a wonderful choice of an outfit for her. I felt that it was time for you to start realizing that you were/are overly conscious of your weight, so I said, "I think the dress looked really good on her. The idea that you have to be really skinny to wear short skirts is an idea from your generation. People have different ideas now. Many teenagers now don't think it's a shameful thing to show your legs even if they're a little big." I think you took what I said to heart and I'm very glad about that.

I love you so much and I don't want anyone reading this letter to think that you're an unkind or unloving mother. We're a perfect fit for one another and I love you so much. You just have some insecurities —especially about your appearance—and unfortunately you haven't yet been able to face or overcome them. Well, I guess that's what the future is for. I just want you (and everyone else in the world) to realize that there's not just one type of beautiful.

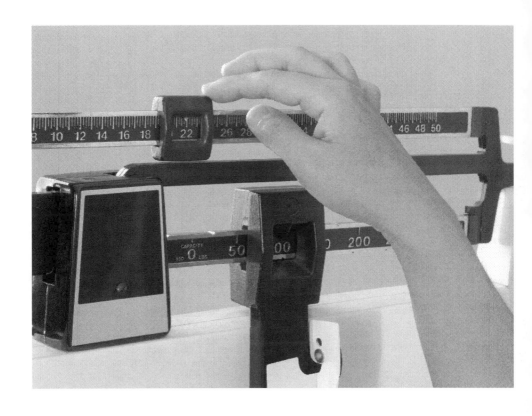

Body Image

Mariana Glusman, MD

Eating disorders affect over 5 million Americans each year. Nine out of ten of them are women. Eating disorders typically appear in adolescence, but may begin as early as age 8. When most people think about eating disorders, they think about Anorexia Nervosa and Bulimia, the most extreme manifestations of distorted body image. But the truth is that the majority of girls and women have body image issues, leading to unhealthy dieting. One study showed that by age thirteen, 53% of American girls were "unhappy with their body." By the time they were seventeen, this number was as high as 78%. Another study showed that 80% of 10-year-old girls have dieted and 90% of high school junior and senior women diet regularly.

Boys are affected too. Over the past three decades, male body image concerns have almost tripled, with 43% of men surveyed stating being dissatisfied with their bodies. In adolescent and college samples, between 28% and 68% of normal-weight males felt they were underweight and wished to become more muscular through dieting and strength training.

We blame the media, and we should—Unhealthy body ideals are everywhere: TV, videos, the internet, and magazines. More than two thirds of girls in one study said that magazine models influence their idea of the perfect body shape. In those who were already dissatisfied with their bodies, prolonged exposure to fashion and advertising images in a teen girl magazine was linked to more dieting, anxiety, and bulimic symptoms.

But, as parents, we also have to look at ourselves. Are we modeling unhealthy eating habits? What is our own body image? An open discussion about body image can start with a question about general facts, such as, "Americans spend fifty billion dollars per year on diet aids, why do you think that is?" Once you are on the topic, the conversation can turn more personal. "Do you know anybody with an unhealthy body image?" Be ready to examine your own beliefs!

I always say one day I will tell

"*I always say that one day I will tell my family.*

Over the years on separate occasions, my mother has asked me if anyone has ever touched me.

I lied every time.

I will probably continue to lie because of the fear I carry.

Here is the Truth

> All these years I have been locked up, chained up inside.
>
> Has that ever occurred to your mind?
>
> Why I never walked away?
>
> Why I played by myself?
>
> Why I comforted myself?
>
> Why I never cry in your presences?
>
> Why I am so quiet?
>
> Why I never say what's wrong with me?
>
> Why I have no group to hang around all the times?
>
> It hurts knowing you are there for me, but emotionally you are not
>
> It hurts knowing I have never had a birth family to care for me
>
> And above all knowing the scars I hold will never be healed
>
> The empty space in my heart will never be occupied.
>
> Hoping one day my family will show up on the corner
>
> But they never show up

I am a single parent

❝I am a teenager and a single parent. *I am still in high school. It is hard to study and raise a child at the same time. Any mother will understand this, but they probably have some help and I pretty much don't have anybody. The baby's father walked out as soon as he learned I was pregnant and my family just keeps saying how disappointed in me they are. I live in my mother's house but I am really on my own.*

Girls make decisions every day that can affect their life forever, like having sex with a guy to feel loved. They can take disrespect, cheating and even abuse because they think he might change. But he won't change. I would like to tell all girls not to lose your self esteem. Believe in yourself and don't let anybody disrespect you.

I could have talked to my mother so many times and didn't. She wanted me to be a success in life and now I have let her and everybody down. Once I made the honor roll. Now I don't know if I will even be able to graduate high school.

Used

"I love how you care

About me

I hate how you

Use me

I feel crumpled up

Thrown away

But then again

You ask

What's wrong?

You hug me

And everything feels

Right

I can just forget

But then

You change

You leave

And my walls

Go up

To protect me

Just stop

Using me

You're confusing me

I need you

To help me

To stop

Hurting me

Should I give up?

Or still

Try?

Holding on

Pretending

On the outside

I don't care

But on the

Inside

Being torn up

Or should I

Let go

And try

To forget

How you

Make me feel

When you are

You

Appreciate my Life

Vs. 1

66 *All I want is to sleep at night*
Without thinking about my life tonight
These rumors in the air are like shootings of a flare
It blinds me scared I'm thinking "Who's over there?"
I'm losing all my sleep my thoughts are running deep
I'm lying in my bed and counting endless sheep
While the pillows drenched with every drop of sweat
Like a sinner pardoned, but still yet to repent
These lines on my face getting thicker by the hour
Losing my self when my weakness is my power
Thinking myself to my own self-conceding
Believing the hype when I know I've been cheated
Myself my home is bi-cultural intertwined
I've been living and complaining doped up on red wine
My lungs filled with air I can't take this whole race thing!
It's driving me to face my own self-complaining
I'm facing days in the same old ways
And checking my birthday to see a different sounding name

Vs. 2

66 *Your childhood's like this when you're just a little kid*
They treat you like your last name is Bin Laden
They throw your back against the walls and shoved in bathroom stalls
Your family feels the pain when you ignore their birthday calls
I've stumbled to my room and shut the door in a blaze

People ticked me off when they told me its a phase

Is it true you can't marry unless it's arranged?

And that you all worship elephants and snakes?

No my friends I believe in Jesus Christ

The one who died for us the one who gave his life

The one who placed his head in a crown full of thorns

Awoke the sleeping souls from night until the morn

Soldiers live once they die tragic deaths

I've died twenty times since I've walked my baby steps

Body's broken and banged my mom's eyes full of tears

She wiped my fears while spit coated my left ear

Vs 3

 I lived out of the city but I'll tell you this

Neighborhoods can change when new neighbors move in

White Houses and Presidents; First Ladies reside

Watching their green grass compounding every night

Waiting to be seen on the covers of magazines

And living in fantasies they could never achieve

But then a brown seed came and decided to move in

The flowers that grew were different colored skin

The pots and soil were starting to get too small

Roots burst into Indians shopping in the malls

Leaves were trimmed accents remain the same

Our talk sounds different but we're one in the same

The gardens grew flowers bloomed without any class

Drive cabs with hands and handled food stands

But flowers kept blooming and I'll tell you again

We'll all move ahead when we stand together as friends

As children we are taught

Student, Northwestern University

❝ *As children, we are taught about diversity and encouraged to embrace the differences that make each of us unique. We are distinguished by our race, gender, religion, ethnicity, and even the way we dress.*

How is it then that, in this effort to accept everyone for how different they are, we overlook our most evident similarities? Above all else, we are all human beings and all of us crave love and acceptance. While most teens cannot identify with the experience of living in a refugee camp, like many African kids have done, they can empathize with feelings of solitude and fear and loss. They can imagine, and they can have compassion.

Adolescents across the globe are looking for a safer, brighter future in which they can pursue personal goals. All come across obstacles that prevent them from doing so. We all have uncertainty and anxiety, just some more than others. Whether it is war, poverty, abuse, or illness, teens of different cultures are living in the same world.

In a way, our differences complement our similarities. Our countries may be not agree with each other politically, or may be excluded from global attention, but we, as people, share so much. Thus, it is not surprising when youths from completely different cultures find that they all are concerned about getting a good education, making a difference in the world, or just overcoming some smaller personal anxieties, like problems with dating. When these kids can come together, they do not only speak about their individual lives, they get the opportunity to listen and get to know each other.

When they talk together, and can respect each other's differences, then maybe they can also see their similarities. Hopefully, they can be future leaders and major motivators of change, young people who respect each other's views about living in today's world.

Changes In My Life

"My parents' divorce affected me greatly. It was a dramatic change in my life. My father fled, my family went broke, and I had no direction. I was very close to my father and his leaving made a huge hole in my life.

During my freshman and sophomore years, I lived a very lavish lifestyle, but then my life flipped upside down. I still woke up every day, went to school, and saw the same faces, but nothing was really the same-except for the teachers who continually encouraged me to keep on going and stay on track. School was not easy for me, but I am sharing these personal feelings now because I decided to let everyone know what a wonderful place a high school can be. I've graduated and moved to another state and am living with a family there. I attend Community College. Recently I was able to see my father and I reflected on my life. After giving the last several years a lot of thought, I just want to say thank you to some of my family and some people at my first high school for being there for me when I really needed you, especially my wonderful teachers who had so much confidence in me. It really made a difference. I'm OK. Thanks."

At home when everyone is yelling

"*Lately, I have been coming home later and later to avoid my parents' yelling. It wears me down. I want to be out of my house but I don't know where to go.*

What do I wish they knew? I wish they knew I was a real person and I wish they could just make peace or get a divorce. Living like this is horrible for them and for their kids too."

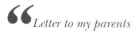*Letter to my parents*

It's different not living with your parents - even if the people you are living with are relatives. I've done so many rotten things that I regret and wish I had never done. It is because you didn't let me make any choices, so when I got the chance to make a choice, I ended up making some wrong ones. Also, you were too strict with me. So every chance I got to feel good about myself and not be depressed, I took. Even when it came to taking drugs.

It's not good to be too strict on a teenager, because the teen years are the years a child gets to learn about life. How can they learn if they are bottled up all the time? Ever get the feeling that you just need to get out of the house because if you stay any longer inside it you might just turn crazy? Well, we feel that too.

I've turned into somewhat of a promiscuous girl and why? Because I've never felt truly loved by you, so I yearn for attention and will do just about anything to receive it. Even when sometimes it isn't the right attention.

By doing so, I played the one guy who did truly love me, and now he won't even speak with me. I didn't notice just how much of an effort he put in our relationship till the day he had enough.

I've gone through so much already and I wish you would just pick up the phone and call me and listen to what I've been through. But it seems as if we're too distant emotionally for me to get personal about my feelings.

I wish I could say I hate you, but I don't. I dislike so much what happened between all of us. But I could never hate you. NEVER. There are times when I get angry at the both of you, but it could never become a grudge. Because the past is out of my control and the only thing I can control now is the present and try to be able to create a bright future.

I am proud to say though, that I am no longer that promiscuous girl I used to be. I no longer yearn for attention. If I am not able to receive it then, obviously, I do not deserve it. I want others to give me their time and affection because they feel I deserve it, not because I make them feel I do. I am still heartbroken about that one guy. He was my first true love. But I am getting over it.

I wish I could tell you everything and for you to just listen and not judge me about it. But for now, until we meet again, I will smile and just say I am ok every time you call.

I used to dream about life out of the orphanage

"*Although I was not brought up by my own family, I think being raised by 21st century parents is hard because everyone seems to be more focused on what they do and their own happiness, without caring more for their children or family. I lost my family during the genocide war. I was taken to an orphanage in Zambia led by nuns. And then I came to the United States.*

Coming to the United States was like going to heaven. I used to dream about life out of the orphanage. Although the orphanage received volunteers every year from all over the world to teach us, I never seemed to learn enough about life in other countries because of language problems. These volunteers spoke different languages and I only understood local Zambian language. However, my greatest dream was to travel far and see everything I would never imagine. Then my dream came true. I flew to the United States.

I moved in with a new white family, something I never expected to do. Most of time, I look at myself and I feel I don't belong anywhere. However, I think people that have been part of my life have been a family to me. It is sad to lose the people I love; most ironically, the people that remain have become precious to me. And that's how I feel. Even when I don't feel fully connected with my new family I feel beloved and cared about in many different aspects of my life.

It was in the summer when I met my American "family." The first time I lay my eyes on them, I felt like I was in another orphanage. I said to myself, "these people are white, and how am I going to fit in their family?" My heart trembled! I became so afraid because I did not know how to interact with my new family or how to talk to them. Despite such thoughts creeping in my mind, I have come to like living with them and accepting them as parents.

Over the last years, they have been acting as parents to me by showing great interest in my daily life. For instance, everyday after school they both talked with me to find out how my day at school was. They gave me good advice such as to accept myself and believe in what I can do. Sometimes when I am in bad mood and I don't want to talk to anyone, they always find something interesting to do with me. One time we went to my favorite restaurant even if my new dad didn't like the food. In these ways they have become my parents.

My dad is great

" *My dad is a wonderful father. He knows how to love life and has given me the best example there is.*

What happened?

 *We were like one*

Like two peas

In a pod

We did

everything

Together

But what happened

I barely recognize you

Anymore

Steady Yourself

"*This is not an essay about a triumph. This is an essay about a time I failed and how I learned more from that failure than from any other experience. My sophomore year, my mother was diagnosed with breast cancer. I wish I could say that at the time when my parents and siblings needed me most, at fifteen years old I was the sort of person who could drop everything and help carry my family's burdens. But that would be a lie. My mom got sick, and instead of being the loving, responsible daughter she'd always known, I messed up; I stayed out late with friends, I stopped doing my homework, I tried to be home as little as possible. I misbehaved because I was scared and because I suddenly had an excuse, a crutch to lean on.*

My friend's mom had died of breast cancer two years before and it was terrifying to see my mother in a similar position. I felt lost, powerless, helpless. I felt isolated. My mother's illness was beyond my control. I whined about every little detail of every aspect of my life. I didn't pay attention to how my actions affected the lives of everyone around me. Nothing was working out and everything required more effort than I was willing to give. I'd fallen on the ice rink and refused to get up. The adults in my life knew that I could figure things out, but I wasn't so sure. When my theatre teacher noticed that I was struggling in her class, she tried to reach out to me. I felt patronized. I was sure that I didn't need anyone to lean on or tell me how to handle myself. When my parents tried to reconnect with me, I pushed them away. I only remember pictures of that year. I think back on who I was and it makes me feel sick.

What changed things? Not a sudden epiphany, but a slow realization that I could take charge of my own life and the understanding that although I can't control everything, the things I can control make a huge difference. I didn't stay up one night and realize that things had to change, I thought about it every night for months, filling diaries with fears and excuses, plans and dreams. I started writing poetry again. Through dedication to my family and by getting involved in new extracurricular activities, I was able to gradually regain my balance. I readjusted my jacket, tied up my laces, and brushed the snow off the blades of my skates. My mother was lucky, the doctors had caught her cancer early, and after a mastectomy and reconstructive surgery, she was cured. That's not to say that it was easy, but it could've been so much worse. I was lucky, too.

My mother and I got better together. By the end of junior year, I excelled academically. I truly enjoyed my classes, and loved discussing and debating what I'd learned with my teachers and my friends. I was elected the vice president of the literary magazine club and had the lead in the play. I joined the Luna Negra Dance Company and wrote and painted in my spare time. This year, I've also become passionate not just about reading and writing poetry, but also performing it, and I love being a member of my high school poetry slam team. I've become a joyful, vibrant person who loves to make people laugh.

In high school, all around me there are kids slipping on the ice, making poor decisions, flailing. Having once been in that position, I can empathize when someone is in a bad situation and I have learned not to define people by their mistakes. Now, I realize that it's not just me, everybody has issues, and I'm not the only one with a wet butt. I know that when things get slippery, I can find a way to make it around the rink and have fun in the process. I have learned to ice skate. I'm looking forward to figuring out how to leap and spin and glide on the ice.

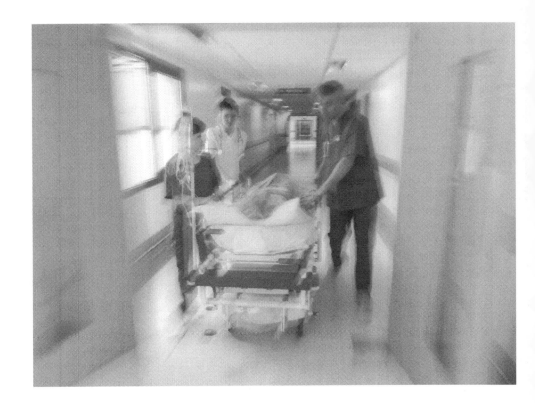

He's Still My Dad to Me

66 *I remember when "traumatic brain injuries" was just a section in my health textbook, and "the fall from innocence" was just an archetype studied in our ninth-grade mythology unit. That was before the accident that left my dad disabled and changed the life of each person in our family.*

I was only twelve years old when hospital visits became a daily occurrence and phrases like "temporal lobotomy" and "inner cranial pressure" became part of my everyday vocabulary. Yet many of the most important things have not changed.

Crash! I jumped off my bike and turned around. A block back, I saw a stalled black Honda Accord, its windshield shattered into a spider's web. From the metal-on-metal clash, I thought the car had hit a stop sign, but as I peddled over, I found a man stretched out in front of the fire hydrant. "You hit a person!" I called out to the driver. The man had a small gash on his right forehead. His eyes were bloodshot and unfocused, and he breathed with an ugly snoring noise. Then I noticed the man's orange undershirt and my heart started racing. It was my dad.

"Dad!" I cried out. "Dad! Can you hear me?" He did not respond. My mom and brothers were far behind my dad and me on our bike ride home; I had been ahead of my dad, a block away from our house, when the car struck him. It seemed to take forever for the ambulance to get there, each second elongated with my dad's life in peril. When the ambulance finally arrived, my dad was placed on a stretcher and loaded in, and my mom rode with him to the hospital. My brothers and I followed in an unmarked squad car. When we arrived at the hospital, we went into the chaplain's room. "My name's Priscilla," she said. We all took a seat. My mom came into the room with the release forms that were handed to her by the doctors. Priscilla, a gentle African-American, asked us what happened.

*"My dad was hit by a car," my brother said.
"How's Dad doing?" I asked.*

My mom hesitantly replied. "The doctors said when he entered surgery, his body was in very good shape." This sugar-coated answer was met with skepticism from everybody in the room.

"Do any of you have a special prayer you would like to say?" Priscilla asked empathetically. Nobody answered. The extent of the damage was starting to settle in.

Friends and family poured into the hospital. The night grew increasingly tense, and I became more impatient. I kept asking my mom when Dad would come out of surgery. Then my mom gathered my brothers and me around her.

"Is Dad going to live?" I asked. She repeated her earlier response: "All I know is that all the biking he has been doing over the past few years has made his body stronger…"

"—Is he going to live?" I interrupted, demanding a definitive answer. "I don't know." Our heads sank.

Finally, the neurosurgeon emerged from the metal double doors at the end of the dimly lit hallway. Everyone anxiously crowded around him. The surgeon's words were strangely impersonal.

"As you know, the impact to the patient's head caused his brain to swell, increasing the pressure in his brain. The team here performed a craniotomy to reduce the swelling. Right now, the patient is in a drug-induced coma, and the staff will continue to monitor the pressure in his head."

One Sunday afternoon, eight weeks later, Dad and I played one of our favorite games in the nearly empty cafeteria of the Rehabilitation Institute. On the thick plastic table stood the familiar yellow-holed panel and blue supports of our shabby Connect Four set, with the red and black checkers scattered across the table. Across from me, my dad was seated uncomfortably in his recumbent wheelchair. An enormous scar arched over his awkwardly titled head and disappeared into his ruffled graying hair. At the base of his neck, a pink hole had formed where his tracheotomy had been, and contusions on his right arm marked former IV tracks.

"Dad, do you want to play Connect Four?" I asked. A hoarse mumble emerged from his dry mouth. I could tell he was not interested.

"Dad, let's play Connect Four," I said assertively as I set it up. I dropped in the first black piece. My dad put in a red piece with a little look of concentration or curiosity or doubt. I took my turn, and then my dad let go of his second piece, not even checking whether it was the right color. I dropped in a black one and then waited for him.

"Dad," I called, "it's your turn." He fell asleep.

Was this the dad I used to spend long summer evenings with, locked in fiercely contested Connect Four mini-tournaments and best-of-eleven series?

One warm evening six months later, my dad and I sat down again to play Connect Four. The object of the game is to create a line of four pieces of the same color. I had already set up the worn out game on the patio, and as soon as my dad wheeled over to our picnic table, we began playing. This time, my dad dropped in the first piece. I followed quickly. Before I knew it, all but one column of the panel was filled up. Our individual colors bordered the empty aisle, sometimes three in a row. "Your turn," I said expectantly. Finally, just two empty spaces remained. The black piece I dropped mixed into the spotted sea of red and black. So did his red piece. Stalemate.

From these games, I knew that life was never going to completely return to normal; however, the changes that my dad underwent from his accident do not change the love and admiration I have for him. Even if he does not walk the same way or can no longer beat me at Connect Four, he is still my dad to me."

Thankful

"*Hi all, I can tell by the number of 'checking in' emails I have been receiving that I am way behind in updating you all on my world and the fight against breast cancer, or as I like to call it, HairWatch. Sorry for the delay. I have been a bit mired in treatment and tired of side effects, (and just plain tired), but here is the latest.*

I have finished 13 out of 16 total chemo treatments. Hard to believe that I am almost finished. I am getting some side effects, like neuropathy (where my hands and feet go numb and tingle) and the fatigue is really kicking in, but my head is covered in peach fuzz and I am sprouting lots of new eyelashes, so that's pretty cool. After chemo I will have my surgery to remove whatever is left (which feels like just about nothing at this point) and then 6-7 weeks of radiation. Hopefully by March I will be through with the bulk of the heavy treatment and will just have the leftover meds to prevent recurrence.

I know I usually tell a funny story about something weird that happened to me because of treatment or cancer or whatever, but given that it's so near that most American of holidays, I thought maybe I would share some other thoughts.

Now don't get me wrong, cancer and cancer treatment can be a pretty thankless experience at times. It hurts, it's scary, you feel like a complete ass from chemo, etc. etc. But (and I know this doesn't sound like crazy, cynical me) I have tons of things to be thankful for right now - some directly related to cancer, and some, just fringe benefit style side effects. Here is a partial list.

I am thankful that my cancer was caught early. I am thankful that my tumor has all the markers so I can have medications to keep me healthy for a long time to come. I am thankful that I live where I do and have access to the best cancer docs in the world, and that my family can afford the treatments that will save my life. I am thankful that I am a candidate for a lumpectomy and that my surgeon cares about leaving me a pretty pair - cause let's face it, they are spectacular.

I am thankful for those of you who have gone on this journey before me and are willing to share your experiences (and hats and scarves) with me. I am thankful for my family and that I have young, energetic parents who take care of me. I am thankful for my sister who doesn't mind spending three hours in traffic just to spend 45 minutes with me. I am thankful for the fact that little kids are honest and open and not afraid of bald people.

And finally, I am mostly thankful for having the opportunity to truly know who my friends are, and how many of you there are. It's very easy to feel sorry for yourself when you are ill, and I admit to more than of my share of self-pity than I should be allowed, but even on my worst days the little voice in my head won't let me forget how many of you are out there, wishing me well, praying for my health and willing to help me in whatever way I need. And that is the most comforting feeling in the world.

I hope that you all have just as many things to be thankful for.

It's okay to be fragile and seek help

"*My dad died. I don't feel the need to go into too grandiose of detail besides to say that it was tragic. Beyond being a successful businessman, he was the type of person everyone wanted to be. He was 45 years old, raising three children, a thinker, dreamer, creator, and passionate philanthropist. So, when he was diagnosed with cancer and taken from us two months later it was, like I said, tragic.*

When he died I was 11, my brother 10, and my sister 7, therefore making me the oldest. My dad was also the oldest so we used to always bond over it. While my siblings and I are very close in age, his only brother was eleven years younger than him, allowing him to take the oldest child role to a whole new level. His favorite story was when on the eve of my uncle's first night of high school my dad said to him, "If you get all A's throughout high school, not even one B, I'll buy you a car." Sure enough, my uncle graduated as valedictorian, not one mark lower than an A, and so my Dad did in fact buy his eighteen year old brother a car. My point is that when he died I felt like I really, REALLY needed to start acting like the oldest. To me, this responsibility meant acting like I could carry on. Sure, I was sad, but it was more important for me to help my younger siblings.

What I wish I knew was that this ideal couldn't be further from the truth. "I was sad" has got to be the understatement of the century. Crying myself to sleep and feeling sorry for myself was what I thought coping was. Bottom line: I wish I knew that it is okay to ask for help. Yes, I may have been the oldest, but let's be real, eleven years old is absolutely still a child. I refused to see the social workers and therapists that my mom, her friends, and my teachers tried to make me go to. Probably because they felt badly for me, they let me have my way, even though they knew I was wrong. Looking back on it, I think so many things about me would be different. Had I talked to someone, maybe I wouldn't have been obsessed with secretly feeling badly about myself. Maybe my often-volatile relationship with my brother wouldn't be that way. Who knows.

The long and the short of it is that it's okay to be fragile and seek help. Had I actually been as mature and eldest-sibling like as I thought I was, I think I would have known that.

Inch by inch,
Row by row,
I'm going to make
This garden grow

“*I think this is from a line in a song. My mother used to always sing it when she did chores. I like it because it makes me remember how determined she was about always making life better. She knew nothing happened all at once. It takes effort. And important things happen a little at a time. And things don't always show while they're growing. My mother was a wise woman. We didn't have a yard or a garden, but we have a pretty terrific family. And now I think I know what she meant. I miss my mother a lot. I wish she was around to read this.*

The Loss of a Parent

Judith Schiffman, LCSW

"Loss of a parent comes in many forms. By young adulthood it is estimated that 15-20% of children will lose a parent through death. Others find their living and home situations changed by divorce, illness, accidents, abandonment, homelessness or violence. Each of these children go through a process of grieving whether it is for the parent they lost, the parent they wanted or the parent they won't have. For most children, it is all of these images of their parent. They are confronted with what they had and expected to always have no matter what the relationship was like.

Children grieve differently than adults. They often move in and out of their grief. As they grow, they keep reworking their loss. Studies have shown us that the loss of a parent is profound and that there are throughout life constant reminders and thoughts about the parent. Often following the loss, the child will take on a characteristic or interest of the lost parent as a way to keep them close.

We need to let children grieve. We need to expect them to be children and not replace the lost parent. We need most of all to allow the child to talk about his loss. Acting as if it didn't happen or being afraid to discuss it only burdens the child more. Our own grief may be overshadowed by how available we are to the child, but we need to learn to be open and honest. It is okay to tell a child you are sad or angry or guilty. He knows it anyway. It also helps him know that there are many different feelings that are evoked by a loss. It helps him feel less alone.

I wanted to be in the hospital

"*I've been searching for a salvation since I was nine years old.
My girlhood was shaped by the media's romanticized portrayal of
depression and mental illness in movies such as Girl Interrupted
and memoirs and novels such as Elizabeth Wurtzel's Prozac
Nation and Sylvia Plath's The Bell Jar. Exposed too early to
popular depictions of psychiatric hospitalization, I formed a
distorted view of hospitalization as being a glamorous, exotic
vacation. As I entered adolescence, this notion stuck with me,
luring me with its promise of redemption.*

*When I was a sophomore in high school, I fell headlong into
what many sufferers have called the "black hole" of depression.
At age 15, my future looked bleak and my dreams seemed
unreachable. Based on the romantic fantasies of my childhood, I
found myself magnetically pulled toward the idea of psychiatric
hospitalization. I thought it would restore the elusive happiness
that lay hidden inside of me. Finally, on a dismal, pallid
Sunday afternoon, my parents admitted me to my secretly longed
for haven.*

*Spending nine days in a psychiatric ward was not the safe
refuge I expected it to be. But it steered me towards some tough
questions I'm still pondering more than a year later. I thought
the hospital would be heaven for me. But I was mistaken,
because it was more like a desolate hell. In that white, pearly
hospital, I felt as though I was fading through the walls, and at
times it seemed as if the staff could see right through me.*

I remember looking in a mirror and not recognizing myself anymore. The hospital taught me I could not run away from my depression and that the hospital could not cure me. I was my only salvation, and it would be up to me to change and help myself.

Before being discharged, I remember looking outside the barred window in my room as I searched for answers. I envisioned myself as a confident, resilient young adult. I dreamt of becoming someone amazing, and I told myself before I left the hospital that I would transform myself. I was determined to evolve into a new and improved teenager. Leaving the hospital was a whirring blender of relief, liberation, and fear. I was being set free from a nine-day lockdown. But saying farewell to the hospital also came with struggles. The difficult questions remained: how do you discover an identity that can endure? How do you recover and start over after falling into the black hole? As the months slipped by, I slowly forgot to ask myself the Big Questions I promised myself I would confront when I left the hospital. Now, more than a year later, I look back. I feel good about myself now, but know that those questions still loom ahead of me.

It's challenging to be everything I wish I could be. How do I transfer what's written in my mind into a tangible personality? I haven't found all the answers yet, but now I have hope that over time, the answers will unfold. I can't expect to find my identity overnight; it will be a life-long process. But I know I have my whole life to keep searching.

Dear Bro

I am writing to you because I want to tell you how we are doing and that Mom and Dad are very proud of you for serving our country. They said to tell you they want you to have safe journey home when you come back.

We hope you are well and pray every day that God will keep you safe from harmful weapons. You are strong and we are proud that you are fighting for our country. May God watch over you and protect you.

Mom & Dad and your friends want you to know that we support you and are praying for you to live and be able to come home.

Look at me

"What do you see?

When you look my way

Look at me

Do you see a friend?

Something beyond

Or something in between

Do you even see?

Me looking your way

What are you looking for?

When you look

Straight

Past me

Something better

Someone cuter

Someone who is not

Just not me

What do you see?

One day you'll see

One day you'll

Notice

One day you'll

Care

Someday you'll realize

I'm more than

Just what you see

From out there

I look at you hoping,

Waiting,

Trying,

To get you

To see me

To notice me

To realize

I'm here and

Always will be

So please

Next time you look

Look at me

Not past me

And see

See what I truly am

Not just

What you think

You see

To see that

I will always be here

Conclusion

This project was a labor of love for many of us, and a long one! It began over a decade ago when a small group of students joined me in discussions about improving communication between teens and parents. Before long our group was invited to speak publicly to groups of parents in schools, hospitals and for the Mental Health Association. We invited some professional guest experts and created a program called, "What's a Parent to Do?" Next was the development of the website, What I Wish Conversations with Teens www.whatiwishyouknew.com

But no matter if we were preparing presentations, creating a website or working on this book for parents, the purpose has always been the same:

- to give teens an opportunity to talk about the experiences of growing up today

- to give parents the opportunity to know more about their children and what their lives are like, and to gain understanding and empathy for them

- to provide a means of initiating frequent, easy and respectful conversations between teens and adults

As time passed we expanded from a small group of suburban teens into a community of young people from different countries. Although the composition of our group changed, our mission remained constant, facilitating better communication between the generations.

After giving much thought to the final pages of this book, I felt that most meaningful would be to share two recent writings from that small original group of teens. They are now young adults.

Labor of Love

Laura Thompson

*W*orking on this book has been a true labor of love for the hundreds of teens and parents who have worked with What I Wish You Knew. While the project emerged from the heartbreak of a tragic teen suicide, it has gained momentum thanks to the tremendous hope and enthusiasm of parents, teens, and teachers and advisors over the past ten years. These contributors and supporters have repeatedly reminded us what is at stake and have been generous in sharing their own stories and unique perspectives.

For me, having begun on this project at age 17, it has also been a tremendous journey in creating what seemed like an unlikely partnership and friendship between a teenager and an adult. That we are friends 10 years later is proof that open communication and a lot of patience really can overcome the gap between generations. We hope that the writings in this book have provided a conversation starter for you and your teen to move beyond "fine" and to begin to unlock all of the creativity, enthusiasm, confusion, hope, depth, and love waiting on the other side.

When I was 17, I wrote the piece called "Fine", a part of which is in the introduction of this book. Here is the entire essay. It is still true.

    "*There is no day than can honestly be described as "fine." "Fine" is the verbal equivalent of the "harmless"* cap of an iceberg the crew of the Titanic saw three hours before their boat lay on the bottom of the ocean. It appears to be straightforward, but hides a ship-sinking bulk of thoughts and emotions beneath the calm surface water. Moreover, "fine" is usually delivered with the misleading teenage tone of voice that covers uncertainties and insecurities with outrage and anger. The tone of voice that accosts the listener, even in a single word, with the questions, "Why are you asking me this? Why don't you just leave me alone?"

"Fine" is a mask. "Fine" hides a C- on a recent physics test, a heart-stopping smile from the cute boy with the locker across the hall, and a fight with a friend that feels like the end of the world. Teenagers are hard to talk to, and they know it (the fight with the friend didn't exactly mirror the interactions they saw on Mr. Rogers as a child). Just the same, though, they need someone to listen to them, to hear their worries about friends and grades, and to understand their fears about getting into the "right" college and finding a rewarding niche in the world of work.

Teens need backup. Parents and kids may have a lot in common (probably more than either is willing to admit) but growing up today is not the same as it was even a generation ago. They understand that parents can't ride in as the knight in shining armor and save the day (and really, they don't want them to…well, not usually at least). They just wish that parents could just listen, maybe sympathize with what they're dealing with, and reassure them that we are fully capable of handling it.

Teenagers are like sailors who find themselves at the end of the ship's plank. They peer past the temporary safety of the wooden plank into the wild ocean of adulthood with wide eyes, terrified of taking that next, big step. Looking back to the safety of the ship, their first home, however, they see it is no longer a place we can fit in comfortably. They must take the plunge.

In a way, teenagers are caught between the two worlds of childhood and adulthood and, for a while at least, don't really fit into either. Navigating middle and high school, they start to make their own decisions (albeit sometimes the wrong ones), and they start to find their own way outside of the protective hold of family. They watch friends change and drift away. They weigh the negatives of drugs and alcohol with their alluring promise of friends to hang out with on the weekends and a group identity. They stress over AP classes and SATs and try to be well-rounded and have impressive extra-curricular activities. They fear failure, and they glance anxiously over their shoulders for signs of the Big Brother-like college admission officers who have come to hold so much importance in their lives.

It feels that somewhere along the path toward high GPAs, Ivy League colleges, and perfect relationships between friends and family, we have lost track of some of the more important aspects of growing up—learning to get pleasure from life, finding identity, and making time to pursue passions.

If only everyone could put everything aside, just for a moment, and simply listen to each other, I'm sure it would be discovered that our days are more than just "fine."

When you have children of your own

Victoria Sandler, MD

*T*hen and now. I contributed to this book when I was younger.

As a new mother now, I gravitate between a state of cool collectedness and that of uncertainty, constantly wondering whether my child will turn out "okay". Every decision potentially impacts my new child's future, which places a heavy burden on even the simplest of choices.

In the mirror, I see the type of worried mother I had criticized as a teen and realize that pretty soon I will be the one standing on the other side of the slammed door, dazed by the mystery of adolescence.

While never really being a rebellious kid myself, I still tested the limits of my parents' patience and struggled with insecurity. Being a teenager was a rigorous fulltime job, complete with dramatic pleas for more freedom, awkward attempts at self-expression, and careful dissections of social situations. Like my teen comrades, I was fighting for my place in the world. I wanted to be understood without having to explain myself, to be successful without jeopardizing my social status, and to be a good daughter without compromising my time with my friends.

As a "good kid" I felt a particular obligation to maintain a certain state of propriety and composure. I even failed at breaking curfew, rushing home just to save my poor mother from a night of misery. I thought I had it "tough".

Adolescence is indeed a tricky time.

As children, we are allowed to make silly mistakes; as soon as we cross the imaginary threshold into adolescence, however, we are suddenly expected to have the correct solution to every difficult situation. How can a group of people so fresh to their novel role be expected to function well together on such short notice? Being held to a higher standard of maturity, understanding, and ambition makes this rite of passage particularly challenging.

Parenting is no easy feat either.

My parents struggled daily with parenting decisions, pushing back to maintain boundaries and questioning my judgment. When I decided to color my hair different colors of the rainbow and to wear clothing that made my body seem amorphous, my mother tried to be supportive without being intrusive. While stressing the importance of self presentation and proper first impressions, she never stunted my attempts at self-discovery. She worried like any good mother would – a lot and often – and was balanced well by my father, who played the "cool" card but must have been running worry laps on the inside. It must have been tough for them to trust that I was truly a good kid, especially given that even the good ones get lost in their values sometimes.

They must have scrutinized every decision, wondering whether they were overly-protective or excessively liberal.

They must have worried much like I do now, carrying the burden of making the "right" decision every time.

Thus it seems that both the teen and parent teams have to play the defensive and neither really has the easier position. When one is enduring the tribulations of adolescence, adulthood and parenthood seem foreign and menacing. However, one quickly takes on the alternate role and the fast approaching adolescence of one's own children become unfamiliar and intimidating.

If only, as teens, we had the foresight to understand the troubles of parenthood

And, as parents, we remembered the challenges of adolescence,,,

Then perhaps we could stop waiting for each other to change. Then perhaps we could communicate more effectively and support each other more lovingly. We could stop worrying about whether we are too rebellious as teens or are too trusting as parents. Maybe then we could look peacefully at our newborn children and just stop worrying. Maybe."

Acknowledgements

Thank you to so many people for their help and encouragement of this project. This book has been a long time coming! My sincere and heartfelt gratitude to the adults on our team, all of the professional guest contributors and especially Dr. Mariana Glusman, Dr. Victoria Sandler and social worker, Kate Mahoney.

And what can I say to so very many students for giving up time you could have been spending doing something else? You were my inspiration!

Kim, Angelique, Gabriel, Victoria, David, Sarah and SO many others, **What I Wish You Knew Conversations** would never have happened without you. I was, and continue to be, touched and impressed by your commitment. You gathered to discuss our book and website in dorm rooms and classrooms, in coffee shops and in meetings at my dining room table. You participated in professional workshops in schools, hospitals and libraries. You shared your honest and heartfelt feelings unselfconsciously and gave advice about what parents would benefit from knowing. You taught me the importance of asking good questions. And you will help many other adults realize the importance of taking the time to really listen to their children. Only the first names of students are listed below, but you know who you are! Never underestimate the impact that your words will have in families.

My sincere gratitude to ALL of you for your interest, help, patience and <u>many</u> contributions.

May there be one less parent saying, "If only I had known..."

Abby, Abraham, Al, Alejandro, Alison H, Alison K, Alison M, Amir, Amy Cook, Amy H, Andrew, Angelique, Ann W, Anne P, Anne R., Ayuel, Barbara, Becky, Ben, Beth, Betsy B, Betsy Lane, Bill, Bobbie, Caitlin, Camp Kesem at Northwestern University, Carl, Carol F, Daniel T, Candice, Caroline, Center on Deafness, Charlie, Chelsey, Claire, Colleen, Conner, Dan M, David B, David F, Dave, Dhanya Puram MD, Doug , Elizabeth, Ella Epton, Emily, Erica, Ethan, Frank, Gabriel, Gail, Hands of Peace, Hannah, Harvey, Helene, Hope, Howard, Jack, James, Jan Keller Schultz, LCSW, Jeff, Jenny, Jeremy, Jerry, Jessica, Jill, Jo Hansen, Joanne, John, Jose, Josefine, Josh H, Josh T, Judith Schiffman, LCSW, Judy, Julia, Julie, Kait, Kate Mahoney, LCSW, Katie Smith, Kathy, Kelsey, Ken, Kimberly Weisensee, Kyle, Laura, Lauren, Larry & Marilyn Cohen, Lawyers for the Creative Arts, Lenny, Leo, Leona F, Linda, Lisa B, Lisa I, Lizzy, Luis, Marcia, Magda Walczak, Mariana Glusman, MD, Marilyn, Mark, Marla, Marta Killner, MD, Marcia, Martin, Mental Health America, Michael McVicker, Mike L, Michael N, Mike P, Mike W, Mina P, Monica, Nancy R, Nancy Y, Natalie A, Natalie G, Nell, Nicole, Nikolas, Pat, Patrick, Paul, Peter, Rachel, Robert, Roberta, Ron, Ryan, Safaya, Sam, Samantha T, Sandy, Sarah, Shira, Stand Up for Kids, Steven, Susan, Tamar, Tom Leavens, Victoria Sandler, MD, Weronika, William, Yama and the countless young people who participate in WorldTeach, started at Harvard and now all over the world.

Made in the USA
Monee, IL
08 June 2022

97683078R00113